Caribbean Food

MADE EASY

with LEVI ROOTS

Caribbean Food

MADE EASY

with LEVI ROOTS

More than 100 'fabulocious' recipes
using easy-to-find ingredients

B Bounty
BOOKS

For my dear mother Doreen and my children Bernice, Zaion, Jo-anne, Nathalie, Tyran, Shar and Danai

Caribbean Food Made Easy with Levi Roots

First published in Great Britain in 2009 by Mitchell Beazley,
a division of Octopus Publishing Group Limited
Reprinted 2009 (twice) and 2010

This edition published in 2011 by Bounty Books,
a division of Octopus Publishing Group Limited,
Endeavour House, 189 Shaftesbury Avenue, London WC2H 8JY
www.octopusbooks.co.uk

An Hachette UK Company
www.hachette.co.uk

ISBN: 978-0-753722-35-0

A CIP record for this book is available from the British Library.

Set in Caecilia

Colour reproduction in the United Kingdom
Printed and bound in China

Consultants Hattie Ellis and Diana Henry
Commissioning Editor Becca Spry
Senior Editor Leanne Bryan
Art Director Pene Parker
Senior Art Editor Juliette Norsworthy
Copy-editor Lucy Bannell
Photographer Chris Terry
Home Economist Sara Lewis
Stylist Rachel Jukes
Proofreader Jo Murray
Indexer Diana Lecore
Senior Production Controller Lucy Carter

By arrangement with the BBC

This book is published to accompany the series *Caribbean Food Made Easy
with Levi Roots* produced by BBC Scotland for BBC TWO

Contents

introduction

'Yu tan deh call' yu wuddah never get come!' ('No matter how much you shout I ain't gonna come!') – those words are legendary in Content. They were my words, the words of a young boy growing up in 1960s Jamaica. What I was saying, or shouting, was a defiant response to a call from my beloved grandmother. She was always calling me. What she was doing was teaching me as much as she could; but at times I saw it as chores. Family and friends always greet me with those words whenever I return to my home village of Howell's Content, in Clarendon parish. When I call to them, they shout back 'yu tan deh…!' and it is always hilarious.

I would be out in the cane fields having some sort of an adventure with my best friend Carlie, maybe plucking away at the downy feathers on a scrawny beeny bud (a very tiny bird), gutting it with a small knife and getting ready to roast it on a stick, while my dear old gran would be calling 'Wellesleeey!' – my pet name – in a beautiful, perfectly pitched voice in C minor 7th, starting low and ending in a falsetto.

She's calling because she wants me to fetch something for her cooking. Even from where Carlie and I are engrossed in dissecting the bird, half its body torn away by the size and force of the huge missile shot from my trusty catapult, we can smell the most inviting aromas coming at us, criss-crossing in the cool Clarendon evening breeze, carrying my gran's cooking far and wide into the nostrils and taste buds of all who live in Content. What the hell is she cooking? And what does she want…?

Probably she's calling for me to fetch some brambles to stoke up the fire underneath whatever it is she's got on, so I'd better go. Beenies don't go very far between two hungry 10-year-olds – and I so loved my gran's cooking – so off I'd run at break-neck speed.

Half of our kitchen was outside on the backdoor steps. We never had any running water and there was no such convenience as an oven. The frying pan would be on and inside it her juicy coconut rundown with scallion, onion, tomato, thyme and fresh callaloo from my grandfather's garden, and with that usually went her golden fried dumplings. I used to love learning how to make dough. She would always give me a piece and I'd watch and copy how she used her thumbs to wrap and overlap the gooey pastry, then form a perfect circular disc in the middle of her palm with a dent in the top. Every house makes a different dumpling, so I suppose my style of pressing my thumb in the top of a dumpling comes from paying attention to how my gran did it.

Lots of people lived in our tiny house, including my grand-aunt Sah Madda and her family, all under the one roof, so cooking would be going on throughout the day and, as I was the regular dogsbody, I was involved quite a bit, getting to touch, smell and feel everything that was brought into our house.

The root vegetables I remember were wild, crispy, fresh… and ugly. A real country carrot is not shiny and ramrod straight like a supermarket carrot – no, it looks like it's been in a fight with another carrot, lost and gotten a few bumps and bruises on the way. These were cooked as soon as they were dug up, retaining their flavour and goodness, or grated for a lovely, refreshing, ice-cold carrot-juice punch.

When Carlie and I were all played out in the blistering Clarendonian heatwave, we would both scuttle off, he to his gran, Mrs Senior, and I to my home. My gran would be waiting with a large mug of homemade limeade, or 'wash' with a big piece of ice floating around in it. Most yards had limes trees and the fruit is so useful for all sorts, especially in that refreshing drink with demerara sugar and a spoonful of honey – it washes down everything. Gallons and gallons of it. Great, too, as a detox tea with ginger in the morning.

My grandfather taught me 'big man tings' such as using a machete or a bill and how to kill a chicken by wringing its neck or chopping its head clean off, then draining the blood so it doesn't contaminate the meat; taking me hunting; riding on his horse-driven dray to cut sugar cane in his huge fields miles away; showing me how to dig correctly for yams and the different names they have (yellow yam, *haffu* yam and *pumpum* yam); teaching how deep the dasheen's shoot buries itself in muddy ground; and he also told me the story of 'why the wasp can make an cone [comb]…but can't make the honey'.

Among the trees, plants and animals he had on his land, I learned all I needed to know as a young, inquisitive country boy. Ackee trees, bananas, plums and all kinds of mangos like East Indian, Julie, Black Mango and my favourites Number Eleven and Bull Tone mangos: just the thought of them makes my mouth water, every time. We used to shimmy up my grandfather's Bull Tone mango tree and eat the delicious and juicy flesh around those giant mango seeds, leaving them hanging there the same way. Isn't that so cool? A bit like how a bird would do it really, with no mess or evidence under the tree! So he would come along, look up, see the half-eaten Bull Tones still hanging on and go 'Dem d'yam birds!', while Carlie and I would be licking our lips and laughing at him from behind the *Lignum vitae* tree.

No one sat me down and explained that one day I'd be leaving all that I knew, that I had a mother and father 5000 miles away who would eventually send for me and that soon I'd be torn away from my beloved gran

TOP LEFT Levi at Tuff Gong rehearsal studio, Kingston

TOP RIGHT With Miss Looluloo and a family friend at Miss Looluloo's house in Content

BOTTOM Catching some rays in front of the Roots FM mural in Cockburn Pen

TOP LEFT Boat fishing in Portmore, Jamaica

TOP RIGHT Levi in May Pen

CENTRE LEFT Levi's friend Moonie

BOTTOM LEFT Juice-carton truck

BOTTOM RIGHT Levi cooking dumplings

and my idyllic country life to travel on an iron bird and be force-fed baked beans! Ahhhhhhh!

If my grandparents were both alive now I would be cooking them mackerel with green bananas while telling how I set up my mobile 'Rasta'raunt' at the Notting Hill Carnival and the saga of how I slayed Dragons on the BBC, inspired by gran and with just a guitar and a song.

Gran, you'd be so proud because your inspiration has taken me from being King of the Hill to Cool in the Den. What she taught me I now want to bring to this book, and she's still around watching me go.

the caribbean kitchen

Seek out the wonderful foods and flavours of the Caribbean and explore the islands from your kitchen! Here's a guide to help you find your way. The recipes in my book mainly use ingredients available on every high street. For a very few, you may have to venture out to a corner shop, market or specialist store, but it will always be well worth it.

Ackee

Ackee is used in savoury dishes though it is actually a fruit, not a vegetable. It's the national fruit of Jamaica, and saltfish and ackee is the national dish. You won't find fresh ackee in the UK as, when raw, parts of it can be poisonous. But you can buy it ready prepared in cans and it's worth seeking out. People often say the texture is a little like scrambled eggs – they also call it 'vegetable brains' – and when you mix ackee with its natural partners, such as saltfish or okra, the taste and unusual texture really come alive. It is delicate, so treat it with respect and be careful to keep the creamy curds whole when you mix them in with other ingredients.

All-purpose seasoning, which is also called Caribbean seasoning, is the one ingredient you'll find in every Caribbean kitchen cupboard. It does what it says on the can: it has lots of herbs and spices in it – usually salt, chilli powder, onion powder, coriander, thyme, allspice and black pepper, though the ingredients can vary – avoid buying any that contain MSG (monosodium glutamate). Use it to marinate meat, fish and vegetables, or add it to a pot for extra ready-made flavour.

Allspice is what we call pimento in Jamaica, where it is predominately grown. The name 'allspice' was coined by the British when they arrived and discovered the berry but couldn't fathom its flavour. Then someone said it tasted like all the known spices together and that is how it got its name. You can buy it as a berry and in powdered form. I like to put it whole in porridge and soups and use the powder to season up meat and fish.

Angostura bitters are a mixture of herbs and spices made in Trinidad and, in my childhood, were mostly used in sweet dishes such as cakes. In this book I've also used them for savoury foods. If you can't find the distinctive bottle with the oversized label in the supermarket, try an off-licence, because bitters are also used in the old-fashioned 'pink gin' cocktail.

Spices

Bananas Caribbean bananas are the small, yellow fruits that are familiar around the world, and they are worth seeking out for their special sweetness. But green bananas are also a valuable in island recipes; they are more starchy and are used in cooked dishes. They need to be soaked and peeled very carefully (for instructions *see* Green Banana and Celery Soup, page 43).

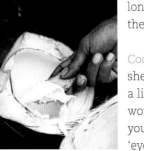

Callaloo

Barbecue is a very Caribbean way to cook; whenever I get my barbecue out I feel like I'm going to a Carnival! In the Caribbean and at Carnival you see the drum pans we use as barbecues on every street corner, with smoke and fantastic fragrances billowing out. The type of wood determines the flavour of the food; you might have someone using hickory wood next door to someone using pimento, and you'll only know which you prefer after you've tried both. What you spray on the fire also determines the flavour. Some people use Irish stout mixed with water.

Butterfish is very popular in Jamaica. It is soft-fleshed, beautifully white and when cooked the right way just melts in the mouth. Try whiting as a substitute.

Callaloo are greens that grow in every garden in the Caribbean: drop the seeds anywhere and up they will sprout. Callaloo is fantastic with saltfish and Scotch bonnet chilli. Summer is a good time to find the fresh leaves in markets (you don't use the stalks) or, failing that, use fresh spinach. You can buy it in cans, but fresh is better.

Christophene or cho-cho, as it is known, is a squash, one of the undiscovered beauties of Caribbean cooking and much appreciated by those who know its magical properties. It has a great texture: always refreshingly melony-juicy and crunchy when raw or lightly cooked; silky smooth when added for a longer time to a soup or stew. You need to peel it and remove the stone, then chop it up how you like, into slivers, slices or chunks.

Jelly coconut

Coconuts are crucial in Caribbean food and every bit is used, even the shells for cups, bowls and to hold dipping sauces. I've known people make a living from the shells, even varnish them to make hair clips that look wonderful. Nothing is wasted when you are a coconut entrepreneur! Did you know a coconut has three eyes but only one? (You'll find three black 'eyes' on the top of each fruit, but you can only get inside through one of them.) So guess which one! Then poke a small knife through it, pour out the juice and drink it (*see* Heart Juice, page 184). Smash it open by banging it against a hard surface, such as an outside wall or step, or put it in a bag and smash it with a hammer: good stress relief! Prize out the flesh with a small, sharp knife, then use it as you want: cut it into very thin slivers in a salsa, grate it for cakes and puddings, or grate it, soak it in water and squeeze it out to make fresh coconut cream or milk. You can also buy coconut milk in cans in supermarkets. I like using just the thicker layer that rises to the top of the can (this is coconut cream), or you can mix the thick and thin parts together for a slightly less rich liquid. Another way to enjoy the wondrous fruit is as blocks of creamed coconut, which you chop or grate to add to liquid ingredients. Coconut cream can also be bought in tubs.

Curry Indian people are represented big time in the Caribbean and their influence has given curry to the repertoire of the islands. I grew up with the aroma of curry coming from the home of our Indian neighbour and Curry Goat (*see* page 24) has become one of the most famous Caribbean dishes.

Dumplings, or 'tumplings' as I've called them in this book, are both the chips and the bread of the Caribbean. You never need to be out of either if you've got a bag of flour in your cupboard, some water in your tap and a little oil for frying. If there are kids at home it costs almost nothing to keep them happy: just make them some dumplings. Cut them open and add anything you want. You can even play cricket with them!

Escovitch is a vinegar-based marinade and sauce often used with fried fish and vegetables in a tropical version of what Europeans call *escabeche*.

Goat is a wonderfully characterful meat and very tender, melting in your mouth. Seek it out and you'll wonder why you've never had it before. You can often find it in halal butchers, or use mutton or lamb as a substitute. In the Caribbean, goat is eaten at big celebrations and even the head is cooked to make Mannish Water, a very famous aphrodisiac soup. I looked after our family goats when I was a boy; we had about 30 and they all had names.

Dumplings

Hard-dough bread is one of my favourites and you'll find it in Caribbean shops. It is white, slightly sweet and has a robust crumb that makes a great chunky cheese and chutney sandwich. The crusts are always prized; indeed, you can pick out the crumb inside and fill the hollow crusty shell with curry goat or even banana.

Ital is vital. Ital is a Rasta's way of saying he lives by nature. Ital is a way of life. Ital is who you are; a Rasta's concept of clean

Okra

living. You will find a number of ital recipes in this book: they will be for really good, healthy food. In the Caribbean, vegetables and fruit come straight from the ground to the pot and are full of fresh goodness: very ital – vital!

Jerk originally meant the way you smoked and cooked food in a barbecue, but now refers to a type of seasoning, a hot mixture of herbs and spices (*see* Sticky Jerk Wings with Sugared Oranges, page 94). Simply rub it on your meat or fish, cook in the oven and savour the magnificent aromas and fantastic tastes.

Limes are used rather than lemons in Caribbean food. When I was a boy we were often given the job of softening the limes, rolling them round and round and throwing them to each other to make them soft and juicy. Working them like this is still the way to get the most from a lime, so roll them on your worktop before using, or get your kids to do it.

Okra is one of those foods many kids don't like, because of its gelatinous texture, but adults love the elegance of this green vegetable. If you steam the slim fingers of okra, rather than boiling them, you will find them juicy and unchallenging. I like to eat them in soups, stews and with saltfish. In Jamaica, they're also served in healthy vegetable smoothies.

Plantain Though they look similar to bananas, you always need to cook large, green, starchy plantain, and it can be eaten in so many ways: fried, baked, in ital food, even with porridge. You can eat it green, when it will be very savoury, or nice and matured with blackened skin; I often buy plantain, then keep it around for a few days to ripen and sweeten.

Red snapper is one of the fish most identified with the Caribbean and it's a favourite of mine. I like the big fish: small snapper means bones but big snapper signifies meat! In the Caribbean we'd chop the head off, boil it up and strain it to make fish tea, so you get two meals from one fish. As an alternative to a big snapper you might try a beautiful turbot.

Rum is the main spirit of the Caribbean, made from sugar cane. Buy white rum or dark rum or, if you are brave and in Jamaica, find yourself a bottle of extra-strong 'overproof' rum that you shouldn't drink while smoking or near naked flames.

Red snapper

Scotch bonnet chillies

Saltfish is the friend of ackee in the national dish of Jamaica. You can buy it dried, either in its original form as a massive cod, or in chunks, and it will need soaking and rinsing to remove excess salt, skin and bones (*see* Saltfish and Okra Stuffed Sweet Potato, page 141). For an easier life, you can also get it in easy-to-use, ready-prepared strips.

Scotch bonnet is the chilli of the Caribbean. It comes in the traditional Caribbean colours – green, gold and red – and the green ones have the most robust skin and are the ones I'd drop whole into a dish. Scotch bonnet chillies are extra hot so I tend to remove the seeds, especially if there are children at the table, but leave them in if you like hot food. And it isn't just about heat; the chillies have a wonderful fruity flavour that is distinctively Caribbean. Remember not to touch any sensitive body parts – either your own or anyone else's – after preparing them!

Sweet potatoes are the main potatoes of the Caribbean; the other kind we call 'Irish potatoes'. I use orange-fleshed sweet potatoes in lots of the dishes in this book, though you can also use the white-fleshed varieties. If you're not sure which you have found in a shop, simply scrape the skin lightly to reveal the colour beneath.

Tamarind was always eaten straight off the tree as a sour fruit when I was growing up in Jamaica. These days you can get it in many forms: whole, in a block of paste, or in jars. Jars are most convenient and it's this type that I've used in my recipes.

Tilapia is a firm-fleshed fish that can now be successfully farmed, and is very tasty. You will find it sold as convenient boneless fillets with a good flavour and meaty texture.

Vanilla is a flavour that no Caribbean home is without. You can use the whole pods or the essence. It's also worth looking around for a mixed essence of vanilla, almond and lemon that can be delicious in porridge and other dishes.

Yams come in different forms, but my favourite is the yellow yam, with its rich texture and sweetish flavour. When you cut it, the flesh immediately turns orange and oozes juice (simply cut off the discoloured part when you want to use the rest). This is the proper yam to add to a Pepperpot (*see* page 27).

Yam

One Pot & Suppers

This is one of my favourite dishes in the book – a real winter-warmer for cold weather, and fabulocious in the summer too. Sweet potatoes are a Caribbean staple and the orange ones are a great colour in this dish, but you could use parsnips instead. Serve it with fluffy Pumpkin Rice (*see* page 123). Fantastic!

caribbean lamb shanks

Serves 4

2 tbsp sunflower or groundnut oil
3 banana shallots or 2 onions, chopped
2 garlic cloves, finely chopped
3 carrots, cut into long, thin slices, about ½cm (¼in) thick
4 lamb shanks
2 tsp crushed allspice
salt and pepper
200ml (7fl oz) red wine
300ml (½ pint) beef stock (see page 188)

500g (1lb 2oz) sweet potato, peeled and cut into 5cm (2in) chunks
2 tbsp tomato purée
2 bay leaves
2 hot chillies (ideally Scotch bonnet or red Thai bird's eye), 1 cut in half
1 cinnamon stick
3 sprigs of thyme
2 tbsp fresh coriander leaves, to garnish (optional)

1. Preheat the oven to 160°C/325°F/gas mark 3. Wash the meat and pat it dry with kitchen paper.

2. In a large, lidded casserole dish, heat half the oil. Add the shallots, onions, garlic and carrots and cook gently to soften for 5–10 minutes, stirring occasionally.

3. Meanwhile, season the shanks by rubbing with the allspice, salt and pepper. Heat the rest of the oil in a large frying pan. Thoroughly brown the shanks on all sides. Add the browned shanks to the softened vegetables.

4. Deglaze the frying pan with the red wine and stock by adding the liquids and stirring until any brown residue from the shanks dissolves. Add this liquid to the casserole dish.

5. Add the rest of the ingredients (apart from the coriander) to the casserole dish and stir it all around. Put a lid on the casserole and put in the preheated oven. Cook for 2½ hours, or until cooked through, stirring occasionally. Served sprinkled with fresh coriander, if you like. Fantastic!

Here is the dish that I'd cook for my grandmother if she were to walk through the door. I'd pour some of the stout in the dish and give the rest of the bottle to her to drink as it was a favourite of hers. This is an interesting combination of flavours – sweet, hot and bitter. Caribbean stout is sweeter than Irish, so if you're using the Irish black stuff, you'll need to add sugar.

levi's homecoming lamb

Serves 2

4 equal-sized pieces of lamb rump
   (about 500g/1lb 2oz in all)
3 tbsp sunflower or groundnut oil
125ml (4fl oz) Jamaican stout, or Irish
   stout mixed with 1½ tbsp soft dark
   brown sugar
mint sprigs, to garnish
Rice and Peas (see page 120), to serve

FOR THE SPICE PASTE
leaves from 3 sprigs of thyme
3 tbsp finely chopped mint leaves
2 spring onions, green part only,
   chopped
½ hot red chilli (ideally Scotch bonnet),
   deseeded and finely chopped
6 allspice berries
juice of 2 limes
salt and pepper
1 tbsp olive oil

1. Wash the meat and pat it dry with kitchen paper. To make the spice paste, pound all the ingredients in a mortar and pestle, grinding it as hard as you can. Mix with the lamb in a bowl, using your hands to get it well coated. Cover and leave for at least an hour, or overnight, in the fridge.

2. Heat the oil in a medium heavy-based saucepan and, when it's very hot, add the lamb. Immediately put a lid on and turn the heat down to medium. Cook for 5 minutes.

3. Swish some water (about 75ml/2½fl oz) round the bowl in which the lamb marinated and add this to the pot. Cover once again and cook for another 5 minutes. Now take the lid off, add the stout and bring to the boil. Immediately turn the heat down low and cook for about 8 minutes, or until cooked through. The cooking juices should evaporate, leaving you with a lovely, dark, glossy stew with a bitter, hot and sweet flavour.

4. Garnish with mint sprigs and serve with Rice and Peas.

This is an adaptation of a recipe from the French Caribbean islands that appears in *The Best of Caribbean Cooking* by Elizabeth Lambert Ortiz. 'Carry' is the same as 'curry'; though in this case the dish has no heat, only beautiful softly scented spices in a coconut sauce. It is very easy to make and you don't even need to brown the meat first.

lamb carry

Serves 4

30g (1oz) butter
1 onion, chopped
2 garlic cloves, finely chopped
400g can chopped tomatoes
2 sprigs of thyme
1 bay leaf
2 cloves
½ tsp grated nutmeg
½ tsp ground cinnamon

salt and pepper
900g (2lb) lean lamb, cut into 3cm
 (1¼in) chunks
200ml (7fl oz) chicken stock
 (*see page 189*)
400ml can coconut milk
150ml (¼ pint) double cream
2 tbsp lime juice
Rice and Peas (*see page 120*), to serve

1. Wash the meat and pat it dry with kitchen paper.

2. Melt the butter in a large, lidded casserole dish – or you could use a Caribbean duchy pot. Soften the onion and garlic in the butter. Add the tomatoes, thyme, bay leaf, cloves, nutmeg, cinnamon and seasoning. Cook, stirring occasionally, for 5 minutes.

3. Add the lamb and cook for 3 minutes, stirring. Add the stock, coconut milk and cream. Cover, bring to the boil, then lower the heat and simmer for 2–2½ hours, until the meat is completely tender and cooked through.

4. Add the lime juice, cook for another minute or two and check for seasoning. Serve with Rice and Peas.

I couldn't write this book without including this Jamaican classic. It can be difficult to get goat, but lamb and mutton are delicious too. Do try to get goat, though – you'll wonder why you haven't tried it before. This has an unusual cooking technique that we use a lot in the Caribbean: steaming and frying at the same time.

curry goat

Serves 4

1kg (2lb 4oz) lean goat meat
juice of ½ lime
2 tbsp mild curry powder
2 tbsp all-purpose seasoning
6 tbsp sunflower or groundnut oil
425ml (¾ pint) vegetable stock
 (see page 189)
1 onion, roughly chopped
2cm (¾in) piece of root ginger,
 finely chopped
1 hot red chilli (ideally Scotch bonnet),
 seeds left in, chopped
2 garlic cloves, finely chopped
10 allspice berries
½ red pepper, deseeded and cubed
½ green pepper, deseeded and cubed
2 spring onions, green part only,
 roughly chopped
2 tbsp chopped flat-leaf parsley
2 tbsp chopped fresh coriander
salt and pepper
2 waxy potatoes, cut into chunks
boiled rice, to serve

1. Wash the meat and pat it dry with kitchen paper – it's fine if there are some small bones in it as they're good for the flavour. Cut it into large chunks, then put it in a large bowl with the lime juice, curry powder and all-purpose seasoning. Turn it over with your hands to get it well coated. Leave to marinate for 4 hours in the fridge.

2. Heat a large non-stick casserole or heavy-based saucepan until it is very hot, then add the oil. When the oil is very hot, put the goat in and turn the chunks over with a wooden spoon to coat the meat in oil. Cover with a lid, turn the heat right down to very low and leave it to just simmer for 45 minutes. The goat will sweat in its own gravy, locking in all the juices with none of the usual browning or boiling – this is the way it's done! Keep checking the pot to make sure the meat isn't getting scorched on the bottom.

3. After 45 minutes, add 150ml (¼ pint) of the stock, bring to the boil, turn the heat right down, cover and leave again to just simmer. After another 45 minutes, repeat this with another 150ml (¼ pint) of stock and cook for another 45 minutes.

4. Add the onion, ginger, chilli, garlic and allspice and stir gently. Add the rest of the ingredients – except the potato and rice, but including the rest of the stock – and bring to the boil. Turn the heat down again, cover and cook for another 2 hours, stirring from time to time. Keep an eye on it and add more stock if it seems dry. Twenty minutes before the end of cooking time, add the potatoes and gently stir them in. Once the potatoes are soft, check the curry for seasoning and serve with boiled rice.

Here's a real classic. Traditionally it would be made from salt beef, but I've used ordinary stewing beef. You could also make it with 950g (2lb 2oz) chicken drumsticks and thighs, each chopped up into small pieces. My pepperpot recipe has ginger warmth as well as chilli heat. The dumplings are optional, but I'd always have them.

pepperpot

Serves 8

600g (1lb 5oz) well-trimmed stewing
    beef, such as shin
1.2 litres (2 pints) beef stock
    (see page 188), or water with
    2 tsp yeast extract
4 sprigs of thyme
10cm (4in) piece of root ginger, very
    finely sliced
1 onion, roughly chopped
1 garlic clove, finely chopped
1 bay leaf
6 allspice berries
salt and pepper
450g (1lb) yam or potato
400g (14oz) sweet potato
450g (1lb) pumpkin or butternut
    squash
4 large spring onions
2-4 hot red chillies
    (ideally Scotch bonnet)
400ml can coconut milk
400g can butter beans, drained
150g (5½oz) spinach or callaloo,
    washed, destalked and shredded

FOR THE SPILLERS' DUMPLINGS
150g (5½oz) plain flour
pinch of salt
4-5 tbsp water

1. Wash the meat and pat it dry with kitchen paper. Cut it into pieces about 1.5cm (⅝in) square and put it into a large flameproof casserole or heavy-based saucepan with the stock or water, thyme, ginger, onion, garlic, bay leaf and allspice, then season. Bring to the boil, skim the froth from the top, cover, reduce the heat and simmer for 30 minutes for beef and 15–25 minutes for chicken.

2. Peel the yam, sweet potato and pumpkin. Cut the yam into pieces the size of large chips. Cut the sweet potato and pumpkin into chunks, about 4cm (1½in). Discard the pumpkin seeds. Bash the spring onions with a heavy knife to release their flavour. Dice the chillies. Put the vegetables in the pot with the coconut milk and beans, stir and simmer gently, covered, for another 25–35 minutes until the meat and vegetables are tender and cooked through. Add the spinach or callaloo about 13 minutes before cooking time is up.

3. Meanwhile, make the dumplings, if using. Mix the flour and salt, then stir in the water and form it into a dough. Pull off about 24 small pieces of dough one at a time and roll them into rounds or long, pointy-ended ovals. (If you want bigger dumplings, use a double-size piece and roll it into a round, putting a small indentation in the top with your thumb.) Put the dumplings into the pot immediately after rolling, about 8 minutes before the cooking time is up (larger ones will need about 12 minutes). We call them Spillers' Dumplings, perhaps because they spill over the top of the full dish of Pepperpot, so make sure the pot is covered. Taste and add extra seasoning if necessary.

This is a great Sunday lunch and reminds me of a cooking technique we use called 'corning', which is when you lay out the meat, season it well, roll it up and leave it so it is really well flavoured. The marinade is just brilliant and you could also try it for roast lamb or chicken.

jamaican pot roast

Serves 6

1.8kg (4lb) topside of beef
4 sprigs of thyme
2 garlic cloves
2cm (¾in) piece of root ginger,
    finely chopped
1 red chilli, deseeded and
    finely chopped
2 spring onions, green part only,
    chopped
2 tbsp soy sauce
2 tbsp malt vinegar
3 tbsp soft dark brown sugar
2 tbsp sunflower or groundnut oil
salt and pepper
1 onion, roughly chopped
1 stick of celery, diced
2 plum tomatoes, chopped
150ml (¼ pint) beef stock,
    plus extra for topping up,
    if needed (see page 188)
4 carrots, scraped and cut into
    chunky rounds
10 small waxy potatoes, peeled

1. Wash the joint of beef and pat it dry with kitchen paper. With a sharp knife, make small, deep incisions all over the meat. Now put the leaves from 2 of the sprigs of thyme, the garlic, ginger, chilli and spring onions either in a mortar and pestle or into a mini blender and work to a chunky paste. Push this into all the slits in the beef.

2. Mix the soy sauce, malt vinegar and sugar and rub it all over the outside of the beef. Cover lightly and put the joint into the fridge to marinate for at least 4 hours, though overnight is even better. Turn the joint every so often.

3. Heat the oil in a casserole that has a lid. Wipe the wet marinade off the beef with kitchen paper, otherwise it won't brown. Season the meat and brown on all sides. Remove the meat and add the onion and celery to the pan. Cook on a medium heat until soft, then add the tomatoes, stock, the rest of the thyme and any leftover marinade from the meat. Bring to the boil, pop the meat back in and immediately turn the heat right down.

4. Partially cover the pot with a lid and let it simmer for 2 hours 45 minutes, or until cooked through, turning the joint over halfway through and topping up with a little extra stock, if needed.

5. Forty minutes before the end of the cooking time, add the carrots and potatoes, replace the lid and cook until they are tender. Check for seasoning and serve the beef in the pot in which it has been cooked.

In this delicious and beautiful dish you get the full diversity of the Caribbean kitchen, encompassing such ingredients as papaya, aubergine, mango and even tamarind. This is a dish for a party! Make it as hot as you want by adding more chilli. In the Caribbean it would be served hot, hot, hot!

martinique coconut chicken curry

Serves 6

4 tbsp sunflower or groundnut oil
salt and pepper
12 chicken pieces (a mixture of thighs
   and drumsticks)
2 onions, roughly chopped
500g (1lb 2oz) butternut squash,
   peeled and cut into 5cm (2in) cubes
2 aubergines, cut into 4cm (1½in) cubes
2-3 large waxy potatoes, peeled and
   cut into 4cm (1½in) chunks
400ml can coconut milk
300ml (½ pint) chicken stock
   (see page 189)
1 tbsp tamarind paste
3 small bay leaves

1 large ripe mango, peeled and chopped
   into 5cm (2in) chunks
1 large ripe papaya, peeled and sliced
juice of ½ lime
1½ tbsp rum (optional)
boiled rice, to serve

FOR THE SPICE MIX
¼ tsp ground turmeric
1 tsp ground coriander
1 tsp yellow mustard seeds
3 garlic cloves, roughly chopped
½-1 hot red chilli (ideally Scotch
   bonnet), deseeded
1 tsp sea salt flakes

1. Pound everything for the spice mix into a paste in a mortar using a pestle.

2. Heat half the oil in a large flameproof casserole or heavy-based saucepan, season the chicken and brown on all sides. Remove and set aside. In the remaining oil, cook the onions, squash, aubergine and potato (if the pan isn't big enough, cook the onion and aubergine first, then add the squash and potato once the other veg are starting to brown). When they are beginning to soften and brown, add the spice mix and cook, stirring, for 4 minutes to release the fragrance of the spices. Return the chicken to the casserole and add all the other ingredients except the mango, papaya, lime juice and rum. Bring to the boil, then turn down to a simmer and cover.

3. Cook until the chicken is tender and cooked through, about 40 minutes. Five minutes before serving, add the mango, papaya, lime juice and rum, if liked. Stir, cover and cook until the fruit is hot. Adjust the seasoning, and serve with boiled rice.

This is one of my favourites. The colours are wonderful and, when you take it out of the oven, you just want to get stuck in. Scrumptious. Similar to Spanish paella, it is a dish that just looks after itself. Don't be tempted to stir – just let the pot do the work on its own.

puerto rican chicken and rice

Serves 4

175g (6oz) basmati rice
3 tbsp sunflower or groundnut oil
8 chicken pieces (a mixture of thighs
   and drumsticks)
2 tbsp all-purpose seasoning
salt and pepper
1 onion, roughly chopped
1 red pepper, deseeded and thinly sliced
1 green pepper, deseeded and
   thinly sliced
2 garlic cloves, finely chopped
6 allspice berries, crushed
1½ tsp turmeric
2cm (¾in) piece of root ginger,
   finely chopped
1 hot red chilli (ideally Scotch bonnet),
   sliced into thin rings (seeds left in)
600ml (1 pint) chicken stock
   (see page 189)
3 sprigs of thyme
2 bay leaves
100g (3½oz) pitted green olives, ideally
   stuffed with pimento
lime wedges, to serve

1. Wash the rice in a large bowl, changing the water until it runs clear. Heat the oil in a casserole 30cm/12in in diameter (if you don't have one, use a heavy-based frying pan). Sprinkle the chicken pieces with the all-purpose seasoning and salt and pepper and brown them well on all sides (you don't need to cook it through at this point). Take the chicken out of the pan and set aside. Add the onion, peppers and garlic to the same pan and sauté over a medium heat until the peppers are softening. Add the allspice, turmeric, ginger and chilli and cook for a minute, stirring.

2. If you are using a casserole, reintroduce the chicken and continue to cook in this. If you are using a frying pan, transfer everything to an ovenproof dish, about 30cm (12in) in diameter; it must be big enough to accommodate all the chicken in a single layer.

3. Pour the rice all round the chicken, pour over the stock, add the thyme and bay leaves and season everything really well. If cooking on the hob, continue to simmer gently over a low heat for 40 minutes. If cooking in the oven, cook for 40 minutes at 190°C/375°F/gas mark 5. When it is cooked all the stock should be absorbed, the top golden and the chicken cooked through (pierce the thickest piece of chicken with a skewer – if the juices run clear, it is done; if not, give it another 5 minutes, then test again). You don't need to stir the rice or cover it or do anything with the dish as it cooks.

4. Scatter on the olives about 15 minutes before the end of the cooking time. Serve with wedges of lime for squeezing over.

What a simple dish, but so full of flavour! Serve it with noodles instead of tagliatelle, if you'd prefer.

gingered-up chicken pasta

Serves 4

2 boneless, skinless chicken breasts, cut into 5cm (2in) cubes
2 spring onions, green part only, finely chopped
4 tbsp ginger wine
juice of 1 lime
1 tsp salt
good grinding of pepper

1 tbsp sunflower or groundnut oil
½ garlic clove, finely chopped
1 hot red chilli (ideally Scotch bonnet), deseeded and finely chopped
2 tomatoes, roughly chopped
75-100g (2¾-3½oz) tagliatelle for each person
olive oil

1. Season the chicken with the spring onion, ginger wine, lime juice, salt and pepper. Let it marinate in the fridge, covered, for 45 minutes.

2. Put a large pan of salted water on to boil. Take the chicken out of the marinade (reserve the marinade) and pat dry with kitchen paper.

3. Pour the oil into a wok placed over a high heat. Add the garlic and chilli, stirring all the time so they do not burn, until you can smell the wonderful aromatic fragrances (about 2 minutes). Take them out of the pan and discard. Add the chicken to the pan and stir-fry until lightly browned. Add the tomatoes and stir-fry for a minute or so. Add the marinade, stir well, put a lid on the wok and leave to simmer on a medium-low heat for 5–10 minutes, or until the chicken is cooked through.

4. Meanwhile, cook the tagliatelle according to the packet instructions. When ready, drain and toss well with a little olive oil, then with the chicken sauce, and serve on 4 plates.

Levi's tip: I like to pour the cooking oil in a thin stream all around the inner rim of the wok so it really coats the pan.

In the Caribbean kitchen we have a cooking technique called 'brown-down' that gets the meat or fish going in caramelized sugar, making a deliciously sweet and savoury dish. This brown-down dish has just four main ingredients, yet it is really special. Kids love it – so does everyone else!

caramel-lime chicken

Serves 3–4

8 boneless, skinless chicken thighs
pinch of salt
1 tbsp pepper
2 tbsp olive oil
2 tbsp granulated sugar

50ml (2fl oz) lime (about 2 limes)
Caribbean mash (see page 116) and
    green salad or Caribbean Griddled
    Aubergine (see page 112), to serve

1. Toss the chicken in the salt and pepper. Put the oil in a large frying pan (it should have a lid) and sprinkle on the sugar. Leave to cook over a low to medium heat until the sugar starts to brown (about 6–8 minutes). Do not stir, or the sugar will clump. You may want to turn the heat up slightly after a few minutes to hurry it along a bit, but keep an eye on it so it doesn't burn.

2. Put the chicken into the pan, turn down the heat and cover with the lid. Cook for 10 minutes, then turn the chicken over, add the lime juice, put the lid back on and cook for another 10 minutes.

3. Check that the chicken is cooked through (pierce the thickest piece of chicken with a skewer – if the juices run clear, it is done; if not, give it another 5 minutes, then test again). Remove the pieces from the pan and keep warm. Stir the sauce, turn up the heat and let it bubble away for a couple of minutes to thicken slightly and come together. Pour over the chicken. Serve with Caribbean Mash and a green salad or Caribbean Griddled Aubergine.

Wonderful ackee is one of the delicacies of Jamaica and a very special food (*see* The Caribbean Kitchen, page 11). It is best known for its role in the national dish, saltfish and ackee, but there are other ways to try it – and I recommend you do! Here it's in a delicious stir-fry that features the bright national colours of Jamaica: red pepper, yellow ackee and green coriander.

ackee stir-fry

Serves 4 as a starter or as a main course with rice and salad

½ tbsp sunflower or groundnut oil
1 garlic clove, finely chopped
2.5cm (1in) piece of root ginger, cut into thin slithers
½ red chilli, deseeded and finely chopped
1 red onion, finely sliced
1 red pepper, deseeded and cut into small chunks

1 tbsp soy sauce
540g can ackee, drained
juice and grated zest of 1 lime

TO GARNISH
100g (3½oz) peanuts (in their skins or dry roasted)
large handful of fresh coriander leaves, roughly chopped

1. Start by roasting the peanuts. Put the nuts in their pinky skins on a baking sheet in an oven preheated to 200°C/400°F/gas mark 6 for 10 minutes, or until they start to brown (don't let them burn!). Leave to cool a little, then rub between pieces of kitchen paper, or in your hands, to get rid of the papery skins. Chop them quite finely, but not to a powder: they give a good bit of crunch to the dish. If you're using dry roasted peanuts, leave out this step and go very gently on the soy sauce later in the recipe, as they are already salty.

2. Heat the oil in a wok and add the garlic, ginger and chilli. Stir-fry for a minute or so, then add the red onion and stir-fry for a couple of minutes. Add the pepper and stir-fry for another couple of minutes. Add the soy sauce, stir well and turn down the heat. Cover with a lid and cook for 5 minutes or so, until the pepper has softened.

3. Very gently stir the ackee into the vegetables. You want the delicate curds to keep their shape, so do not stir them in too much. Divide between 4 plates, squeeze over the lime juice and sprinkle with the grated lime zest, coriander leaves and chopped roasted peanuts.

Soup is a way of opening up your appetite and this one is fantastic at preparing you for more great food to come.

black bean soup with hot roast pepper cream

Serves 6

1 tbsp sunflower or groundnut oil
15g (½oz) butter
1 onion, roughly chopped
1 large carrot, finely diced
1 stick of celery, finely diced
2 garlic cloves, finely chopped
1½ tsp ground cumin
850ml (1½ pints) chicken or vegetable stock (see page 189)
3 x 400g cans black beans, drained

FOR THE CREAM
2 red peppers, deseeded
olive oil
½ hot red chilli (ideally Scotch bonnet), deseeded and chopped
juice of ½ lime
50ml (2fl oz) double cream
salt

1. Brush the peppers with olive oil inside and out and roast in an oven preheated to 180°C/350°F/gas mark 4 for about 30 minutes, or until completely soft. Put the peppers with their cooking juices into a blender with all the other ingredients for the cream. Blend until smooth. Chill until needed.

2. Heat the oil and butter in a saucepan over a low-medium heat and add the onion, carrot, celery and garlic. Cook gently in the fat for a couple of minutes, then add a generous splash of water and cover with a lid. Sweat the vegetables for about 15 minutes, adding a splash of water when necessary to ensure they don't burn.

3. Remove the lid, add the cumin and cook for a minute to release its lovely aroma, then add the stock and beans. Bring to the boil, then turn down to a simmer. Cook for about 15 minutes. Leave to cool, then whizz in a blender until smooth.

4. Reheat the soup and serve hot with spoonfuls of the cream on top.

This is one of my favourites and the sort of food I'd feed to my Rasta friends. It's completely ital and, if you're wondering what that is, 'ital' comes from 'vital', or natural. Make it as hot or mild as you like and change the vegetables according to the time of year. But keep it as pure as possible; I like it with no fat (though sometimes butter's hard to resist) or onions.

ital carrot and sweet potato soup

Serves 4

1 litre (1¾ pints) carrot juice (I juice them fresh in a juicer)
2 sweet potatoes, peeled and cut into 2cm (¾in) chunks
400g can chickpeas, drained
4cm (1½in) chunk of creamed coconut, from a block
1 small hot red chilli (ideally Scotch bonnet), chopped (seeds left in or removed, depending on how hot you like it)
2cm (¾in) piece of fresh root ginger, very finely chopped

1 garlic clove, finely chopped
leaves from 2 sprigs of thyme, finely chopped
large handful of callaloo or spinach leaves, washed thoroughly, tough stalks removed (optional)
chunk of butter (optional)
black pepper (optional)
1 tbsp chopped fresh coriander leaves, to garnish
cream, sour cream or Greek yogurt, to serve (optional)

1. Put the carrot juice in a medium-sized saucepan and bring to the boil. Add the sweet potatoes, chickpeas, creamed coconut, chilli, ginger, garlic and thyme.

2. Simmer gently, covered, for 10 minutes or until the potato is soft. Shred the callaloo or spinach, if using, and add to the soup 5 minutes before the end of cooking time. Leave the soup chunky or smash up the chickpeas and sweet potato with a potato masher if you want. (Adjust the consistency of the soup to taste with a little extra carrot juice or stock if you decide to mash it, as it will become very thick.)

3. Add the butter and season with black pepper, if liked. Garnish with fresh coriander. Serve each bowl with a drizzle of cream or a blob of Greek yogurt on top, if liked.

In my youth, we'd always call an avocado pear simply a 'pear', because that was the only kind we had growing on the island. There was a pear tree in my grandfather's secret garden and he guarded it with his life, along with the mango trees that grew alongside it. But my friend Carlie and I would still pick pears from the tree, bust them open, twist out the stones, devour the flesh and hide the evidence. You don't have to use crab in this recipe, you could also put tomato salsa on top, or just a swirl of cream.

chilled avocado soup with tasty crab

Serves 6

sunflower or groundnut oil
2 leeks, finely sliced
2 garlic cloves, finely chopped
4 tsp ground cumin
1.2 litres (2 pints) chicken or vegetable
   stock (see page 189)
small bunch of fresh coriander
salt and pepper
3 ripe avocados
227ml can tomatoes in thick juice
juice of ½ lime
5 tbsp single cream

FOR THE CRAB
250g (9oz) fresh cooked white
   crab meat
good squeeze of lime
½ red chilli, deseeded and shredded
   very finely
extra virgin olive oil, to serve

1. Heat 4 tbsp oil in a saucepan and add the leek and garlic. Sauté gently until the vegetables begin to soften, then add a splash of water, cover and let the vegetables sweat for about 15 minutes. Stir from time to time, to prevent them catching on the pan, adding a splash more water if needed.

2. Add the cumin, raise the heat a little and cook, stirring, for another minute. Add the stock and the coriander stalks and season. Bring to the boil and simmer, covered, for 15 minutes. Allow the soup to cool.

3. Scoop the flesh from the avocados, roughly chop it, then add it to the cooled soup with the tomatoes, two-thirds of the coriander leaves and the lime juice. Process in a blender, adding another 4 tbsp oil. Stir in the cream and taste for seasoning. Cover and chill for an hour.

4. Just before serving, mix the crab with all the other ingredients, then finely chop and add the remaining coriander leaves. Spoon on top of each serving and drizzle each bowl with a little extra virgin olive oil.

This soup opens up your appetite for a meal to come, or it can be lunch on its own. The greener the banana the better, as it will be more savoury – though it makes them harder to peel. The christophene, which West Indians call cho-cho, is an optional extra in this recipe but it adds a certain refreshing, smooth texture and is worth including if you can find it (*see* page 77 for instructions on preparing christophene). Use as little or as much chilli as you like.

green banana and celery soup

Serves 4

2 green bananas
30g (1oz) butter
4 sticks of celery, peeled and diced
1 green chilli, deseeded and
    finely chopped
½ christophene, deseeded, peeled
    and cut into 2cm (¾in) dice
    (optional)
750ml (1 pint 7fl oz) chicken or
    vegetable stock (*see* page 189)
1 tsp thyme leaves
1 tsp salt, to taste
chunky bread, to serve

TO GARNISH
natural yogurt
leaves from a large sprig of mint,
    roughly chopped

1. Cut the ends from the bananas, cut through the skins down the edges and then put them in a bowl and cover with just-boiled water. Leave to steep for about 15–20 minutes. Put a medium saucepan of water on to boil. Drain the bananas and gently ease them out of their skins, using a small, sharp knife if you need it, then cut into 3cm (1¼in) lengths and put into boiling water in a saucepan. When the bananas are tender (about 5 minutes), drain and mash them roughly: you want some chunky bits and bobs in this soup.

2. Melt the butter in a medium heavy-based saucepan and in it soften the celery, chilli and christophene, if using. Add the stock, thyme and cooked banana. Bring to the boil and simmer, covered, for 15–20 minutes or so, stirring occasionally. Season with salt.

3. Ladle into bowls and serve with a swirl of yogurt and some chopped mint leaves. Serve with the bread (Jamaicans would eat hard-dough bread – *see* The Caribbean Kitchen, page 13) and there you have a meal.

If you are passing by a West Indian market stall, you might try to pick up some tasty callaloo to replace the spinach in this recipe (*see* The Caribbean Kitchen, page 12). It's the equivalent of spinach in the Caribbean and grows in every yard. Take out the stems, chop off the leaves and add it to the pot with the chickpeas.

pumpkin, chickpea and spinach soup

Serves 4–5

15g (½oz) butter
1 tbsp olive oil
1 onion, finely chopped
1 garlic clove, finely chopped
225g (8oz) pumpkin, peeled and cut
   into small pieces
410g can chickpeas, drained

750ml (1 pint 7fl oz) vegetable stock
   (*see* pages 189)
1 bay leaf
125g (4½oz) baby spinach
salt and pepper (optional)
chunky bread, to serve

1. Melt the butter with the olive oil in a large heavy-based saucepan and, in this, soften the onion and garlic over a low heat for about 10 minutes. Add the pumpkin and cook, stirring occasionally, for a further 5 minutes, then add the chickpeas, stock and bay leaf. Cook, covered, for 20 minutes.

2. Remove the bay leaf and roughly mash up the pumpkin and chickpeas using a potato masher to get a textured soup, or whizz it up in a blender in batches if you want it smooth, then return to the pan. Add the spinach, give it a stir and cook for 5 minutes.

3. Check the seasoning, adding salt and pepper, if liked.

4. Serve it up with a chunk of good bread.

This is the national breakfast of Jamaican school kids. It fills everyone up and takes you through the morning. Choose any of the suggested toppings here, but stir it up and start the day!

caribbean porridge

Serves 4

720ml (1 pint 6fl oz) water
10 allspice berries
½ cinnamon stick
good grating of nutmeg
5 cloves
1 bay leaf
400ml can coconut milk
large pinch of salt
175g (6oz) rolled porridge oats

TO SERVE
milk or cream
50g (1¾oz) ready-to-eat mixed tropical
   fruits, chopped, or 2 bananas
50g (1¾oz) pecans, roughly chopped
muscovado or demerara sugar, to taste
allspice berries, to serve

1. Put the water in the pan in which you want to cook the porridge. Add the spices and bay leaf. Put a lid on and simmer for 5 minutes. Now you can fish out the allspice berries and cloves with a slotted spoon if you don't want them in the final porridge. Stir in the coconut milk and salt.

2. Add the porridge oats to the fragrant spiced liquid. Bring to the boil, then turn down the heat and simmer for 5 minutes, stirring often. I don't like porridge too stiff, so I make sure it can still move around the pan, adding milk or more water if necessary.

3. Put the porridge into 4 bowls. Top it with whatever delights you like. Milk is good, cream is great. Chopped tropical dried fruits are colourful, or try banana. I like some pecans for crunch and extra nourishment. Then you can add some sugar, if needs be, remembering your ready-to-eat fruits may be sweetened already. Eat up and get going!

Fish & Seafood

I usually make this with butterfish (*see* The Caribbean Kitchen, page 12), which I get at my local West Indian market. It is a lovely fish that has flesh that melts like butter. But seabass is good too. You should use a big fish as you need a longish cooking time to mellow the spices. You probably feel that rice is the right thing to go with this, but in Jamaica we would serve it with something crunchy, like crackers, scooping the flesh of the fish up on the crackers and tucking right in.

baked spiced seabass with aubergine, spring onion and coconut

Serves 4

2 x 500g (1lb 2oz) seabass, or other
   similar fish, gutted, scaled and
   gills removed
8 tbsp sunflower or groundnut oil
2 aubergines, tops removed and sliced
4 spring onions, 2 trimmed, 2 chopped
8 tbsp coconut cream

FOR THE SPICE PASTE
1 tbsp all-purpose seasoning
1 tbsp mild curry powder
1½ tbsp thyme leaves
1 tbsp tomato purée
juice of ½ lime
salt and pepper

1. Make the spice paste by mixing all the ingredients together.

2. Make 3 or 4 neat slashes on each side of both fish, cutting into them but not down as far as the bones. Rub the paste all over the fish, pushing it down into the slashes, and rubbing all over the insides too. Put in a large dish, cover with clingfilm and put in the fridge for a couple of hours.

3. Preheat the oven to 190°C/375°F/gas mark 5. Heat 5 tbsp of the oil in a frying pan and colour the aubergines (you'll need to do this in batches) until pale gold on both sides. You don't need to cook them right through, just get some colour on them. Season well and lay on the base of a roasting tin or ovenproof dish big enough for both fish.

4. Heat the rest of the oil in a frying pan and cook the fish on both sides, just to colour them a little, about 2½ minutes each side. They should be golden. Set the fish on top of the aubergines in the roasting tin and scatter the spring onions over the top. Now spoon the coconut cream all over the fish and aubergines. Cook in the preheated oven for 20–25 minutes, until the fish is soft, tender and cooked through. Serve straight away.

Lord-a-mercy, this is a great dish! Seabass is one of my favourite kinds of fish and it is so easy to cook in this *escovitch* way (the Caribbean version of what in Europe is called *escabeche*). Prepare it properly (or get a fishmonger to do the hard work!). Remove the head if you don't like the fish to look at you – but I always keep it on: it has lots of flavour, particularly the cheeks. In Jamaica you can tell a lot about a household by how they prepare their fish. We *always* get rid of the gills; if you went to eat at someone's house and the bass still had gills inside, you wouldn't go back.

escovitch seabass

Serves 6

oil for greasing
2 x 1kg (2lb 4oz) seabass, gutted, scaled and gills removed
½ tbsp salt
1½ tsp pepper
½ lime
2 spring onions, trimmed
4 sprigs of thyme
1 hot red chilli (ideally Scotch bonnet), deseeded and thinly sliced
1 tbsp olive oil, to glaze (optional)

FOR THE ESCOVITCH
2 tbsp olive oil
1 green pepper, deseeded and cut into thin strips
1 yellow pepper, deseeded and cut into 2.5cm (1in) chunks
1 orange pepper, deseeded and cut into 2.5cm (1in) chunks
1 red onion, cut into 2.5cm (1in) chunks
1 hot chilli (ideally Scotch bonnet), deseeded and thinly sliced
2 tsp cider vinegar

1. Preheat the oven to 190°C/375°F/gas mark 5. Lightly oil a baking sheet and put the fish on it. Mix together the salt and pepper and use most of it to season inside both fish. Squeeze the half-lime into both cavities as well. Bash the spring onions with the handle of a heavy knife to release their flavour. Put 1 spring onion and 2 sprigs of thyme inside each fish along with half the chilli. Make 3 diagonal slashes through the skin of each bass on the uppermost side only and season with the remaining salt and pepper. Put in the preheated oven and cook for 30–35 minutes, until the flesh is soft, tender and cooked through.

2. Meanwhile, prepare the *escovitch*. Heat the oil in a frying pan over a medium-high heat and stir-fry the peppers, onion and chilli for about 4 minutes, until softened but still slightly crunchy. Add the vinegar and stir into the vegetables for 10 seconds or so. Turn off the heat.

3. When the fish are cooked, brush them lightly with olive oil to make them look glossy, if liked. Arrange the *escovitch* vegetables over and around the fish.

4. I like to eat this straight away, hot; you can also have it at room temperature or cold.

This dish is from award-winning chef Anthony Cumberbatch who has a restaurant, Bamboo Grove, in South Croydon. His family came from Barbados and this is his twist on the national dish.

pan-fried fillet of seabass with tomato and lime salsa and cou-cou (polenta)

Serves 4

juice of 2 limes
2 tbsp fresh coriander leaves
2 tbsp flat-leaf parsley leaves
5 sprigs of thyme
½ tsp ground allspice
1 tsp Worcestershire sauce
1 hot red chilli (ideally Scotch bonnet), deseeded and roughly chopped
3 garlic cloves
3 tbsp olive oil, plus extra for drizzling
4 seabass fillets (about 400g/14oz in total), scaled
75g (2¾oz) plain flour
1 free range egg
2 large tomatoes, cut into 2cm (¾in) dice
2 spring onions, finely chopped

FOR THE COU-COU
600ml (1 pint) water (or 300ml/ ½ pint coconut milk and 300ml/ ½ pint water)
salt and pepper
125g (4½oz) okra, trimmed and chopped into 2cm (¾in) lengths
225g (8oz) coarse cornmeal
30g (1oz) butter

1. Start with the cou-cou. Season the water (or coconut milk and water), with a little salt and pepper, then bring to the boil in a heavy-based saucepan. Add the okra and cook for 10 minutes. Remove the okra, using a slotted spoon, and set aside. Gradually beat the cornmeal into the liquid. Cook over a very low heat for about 20 minutes, stirring to prevent it from burning, until the liquid is thick and smooth. Add the okra halfway through the cooking time. Stir in the butter and adjust the seasoning if necessary. Cover with foil and then a lid to keep the mixture moist and hot until needed.

2. Put the lime juice, coriander, parsley, thyme, allspice, Worcestershire sauce, chilli, garlic and half the oil into a blender and whizz until smooth. Lay the fillets in a shallow glass or ceramic dish and cover with the marinade. Cover with clingfilm and marinate in the fridge for around 15–20 minutes. Do not be tempted to leave the fish for longer or the citric acid from the lime juice will start to 'cook' it.

3. Put the flour on a large plate. Lightly beat the egg in a large bowl. Heat the remaining oil in a large, heavy-based frying pan over a medium heat. Brush off the marinade. Dip each of the fish fillets on both sides in the flour, then the egg, then in the flour again. Cook the fillets, skin-side down, for 2 minutes then turn and cook for a further 2 minutes, until the flesh is cooked all the way through. Add the marinade to the pan followed by the tomatoes and spring onions. Heat everything through (1–2 minutes). As soon as the sauce is hot and the tomatoes are lightly cooked but still have their shape, drizzle a little olive oil over the fish and serve on warm plates with the tomato salsa, accompanied by the cou-cou.

This is a classic and my mum and grandma both made it. You don't have to stick to these ingredients, so use different kinds of fish or try a vegetarian version cooked with aubergine, yam, sweet potato and squash instead of these root vegetables. The traditional use of the word 'rundown' relates to the oil that comes from coconut milk when you boil it up. You scoop it off the top and use it for cooking. Here we're using the very thick coconut cream as it has the same richness.

jamaican rundown

Serves 4

400ml can coconut milk
2 garlic cloves, finely chopped
1 onion, roughly chopped
6 smallish waxy potatoes, peeled
    and sliced
2 carrots, cut on the diagonal into
    thick slices
2 parsnips, each sliced diagonally
    into 6
4 plum tomatoes, deseeded,
    each cut into 8
4 sprigs of thyme
2 tsp malt vinegar
1 red chilli, deseeded and
    finely chopped
salt and pepper
2 whole mackerel, gutted
lime wedges, to serve

1. Open the can of coconut milk, lift all the near-solid curds off the top and put them into a large saucepan. (Use the more watery bit for something else, such as a soup made from squash or sweet potato.) Cook the creamy bit at a gentle simmer until it has the consistency of double cream, stirring every so often to make sure it's not catching on the bottom. This is the 'rundown'.

2. Put everything except the mackerel and lime in a large heavy-based saucepan. Bring to the boil, then turn down to a simmer, cover and cook until all the vegetables are just tender, about 25 minutes. If you find that the mixture gets too dry, add a little water.

3. Meanwhile, cut the heads off the mackerel, then cut each fish in half. Pour the lime juice all over them. Cover and leave in the fridge for about 30 minutes.

4. When the vegetables are just tender, remove the mackerel from the fridge and lay the mackerel pieces on top of the vegetables. Cover again. Simmer for a further 10–12 minutes, or until the mackerel is cooked through.

5. Before serving, you may wish to remove the skin and bones from the fish, then return them to the pan in chunks – or you can leave it as it is. Serve, preferably in the dish in which it has been cooked, providing lime wedges for everyone (it needs a good squeeze of lime on top).

The best breakfast in the world – just ask any Jamaican. Make it with mackerel fillets if you prefer, but don't cook them for so long (only about 4 minutes). It's hard to peel green bananas – here I'm giving you all the banana peeling tips my Granny gave me.

spicy mackerel with green bananas

Serves 2 greedy people

2 whole mackerel, gutted
juice of 1 lime
4 green (unripe) bananas
½ tsp ground allspice
salt and pepper
3 tbsp sunflower or groundnut oil
1 red onion, roughly chopped
2 tomatoes, deseeded and
   roughly chopped
2 garlic cloves, finely chopped
1 hot red chilli (ideally Scotch bonnet),
   deseeded and finely chopped
leaves from 3 sprigs of thyme

TO SERVE
1 tbsp roughly chopped fresh coriander
lime wedges

1. Cut the head and tail from the mackerel and cut the body of each into about 3 chunks. Cover with half the lime juice and leave in the fridge for about 30 minutes.

2. Cut the ends from the bananas, cut through the skin down the edges – north, south, east and west – and then put them in a bowl covered with just-boiled water for 15–20 minutes.

3. Put the mackerel into a medium saucepan and cover with water. Bring to the boil, turn down to a simmer and cook, covered, until completely tender (6–8 minutes). Lift out with a slotted spoon. Remove and discard the bones and skin, if liked, and break the flesh into good meaty flakes. Sprinkle with the allspice, the rest of the lime juice and salt and pepper.

4. Remove the skin from the bananas. It isn't easy and you'll need a small, sharp knife to help you at times, but try to prise it off with your hands. Now put the bananas into a pan with enough water to cover. Add 1 tbsp of the oil to the water and bring to the boil. Cook the bananas, covered, on a rolling boil until tender (it should take about 15 minutes).

5. Put the remaining oil into a large frying pan and heat. Gently fry the onion until softening, then add the tomatoes, garlic, chilli and thyme, season and cook until everything is soft. Add the mackerel, gently stir and heat through.

6. Lift the bananas out of their water with a slotted spoon. You'll notice brown bits on them (though most will be in the water, which will be brown). Brush off any brown bits and cut into diagonal slices. Stir into the mackerel and serve sprinkled with the coriander and accompanied by lime wedges.

This is a simple version of *escovitch* fish (the Caribbean version of what Europeans call *escabeche* fish). You can use whatever vegetables you have to hand; they pickle nicely in the dressing as the fish cooks.

escovitch trout

Serves 4

4 x 300g (10½oz) trout, gutted
    and scaled
1 tsp salt
1 tsp pepper
4 spring onions, green part only,
    cut into 2.5cm (1in) pieces
½ cucumber, cut into long strips
1 red pepper, deseeded and thinly sliced
1 green pepper, deseeded and
    thinly sliced

1 garlic clove, finely chopped
1 hot red chilli (ideally Scotch bonnet),
    deseeded and thinly sliced

FOR THE ESCOVITCH DRESSING
10 allspice berries, crushed
250ml (9fl oz) cider vinegar
150ml (¼ pint) olive oil
salt, to taste

1. Preheat the oven to 190°C/375°F/gas mark 5. Lay each trout on a generous piece of foil (the foil needs to be big enough to make a parcel round the whole fish). Season the trout inside with salt and pepper and stuff in the spring onion to give lots of fresh flavour. Scatter the cucumber, peppers, garlic and chilli over and around the fish.

2. Mix the allspice berries with the vinegar and oil. It is important to use cider vinegar as it has a nice, gentle flavour; you don't want it to be too harsh. Season with a little salt. Pour the dressing equally over all 4 trout.

3. Wrap up the trout, dressing and vegetables tightly in the foil. Cook in the preheated oven for 25 minutes, or until cooked through. Open up the packet and get a beautiful fragrant rush of steam from your juicy cooked fish.

Levi's tip: You can also do this on a campfire or on a barbecue. Turn the fish once or twice while cooking and check after 30 minutes to see if they are done (reseal the foil quickly if they aren't). A lot depends on how hot the embers are and how far the fish are from them.

Kids love this for the luscious coconut and sweet potato mash on top. The colours are great, with the green spinach and coriander, flakes of white fish and orange topping. You could also use prepared saltfish (*see* The Caribbean Kitchen, page 15) or a mixture of saltfish and ordinary fillets.

caribbean fish pie

Serves 4–5

600ml (1 pint) milk
1 sprig of thyme
600g (1lb 5oz) skinned white fish
    fillets, such as haddock, cod or coley
55g (2 oz) butter
2 tbsp plain flour
50g (1¾oz) block creamed coconut,
    roughly chopped
salt and pepper
about 1½ limes, juiced
leaves from a large bunch of fresh
    coriander, chopped (optional)
250g (9oz) young leaf spinach, washed
1 x quantity Caribbean Mash
    (see page 116)

1. Preheat the oven to 180°C/350°F/gas mark 4. Warm the milk and thyme in a saucepan large enough to hold the fish until it reaches boiling point. Remove from the heat and leave to one side to infuse for about 30 minutes.

2. Put the fish in the infused milk. Bring to the boil, turn off the heat and leave to stand for 5 minutes. Remove the fish (reserve the milk) and divide into large flakes. Discard the thyme.

3. Make the sauce by melting half the butter in a large saucepan and adding the flour. Cook, stirring, for a couple of minutes over a low heat. Gradually add the warm milk from cooking the fish, whisking all the time to avoid lumps. When it thickens, stir in the creamed coconut until it melts into the sauce. Season with salt, pepper and lime juice to taste – some may like a stronger taste of citrus in the sauce than others. Add the coriander, if using. Stir in the spinach so it just wilts in the heat of the sauce. Stir in the fish very gently so it stays in the largest possible flakes. Taste and adjust the seasoning if necessary.

4. Put the fish mixture in an ovenproof dish about as big as an A4 piece of paper. Top with the Caribbean Mash and dot with the remaining butter. Put on a baking sheet (this will save you cleaning the oven in case of spillages) and cook in the preheated oven for 20–30 minutes until bubbling hot.

Levi's tip: It's much easier to make a white sauce using hot milk than cold. The milk blends into the flour more easily and there's far less risk of lumps.

The butter on this is so great that you'll want to lick it up with bread – or even your tongue! It is one of my favourite creations and I can't wait for everyone else to try it. It also goes well with Barbecued Lobster (*see* page 143). The salmon steaks are also good with Lime, Chilli and Coriander Mayo (*see* page 126).

salmon with lime, chilli and coriander butter

Serves 4

4 salmon steaks, about 175g (6oz) each
sunflower or groundnut oil
salt and pepper
lime wedges, to serve
Pineapple, Avocado, Orange and Mint
   Salad with Ginger Dressing, to serve
   (see page 107)

FOR THE BUTTER
75g (2¾oz) butter, slightly softened
1½ tbsp finely chopped fresh coriander
1 garlic clove, finely chopped
zest and juice of ½ lime
1 red chilli, deseeded and very
   finely chopped
salt and pepper

1. Put all the ingredients for the butter into a bowl and mash together with a fork. Now scoop it into a piece of clingfilm, wrap carefully and put it into the fridge to chill. When firm enough to handle, form the chilled butter into a sausage shape and wrap in greaseproof paper. Put back in the fridge to chill completely. This way you will be able to slice little round pats of the butter off the roll.

2. Heat a griddle pan until really hot. Brush the steaks on each side with oil, then season. Put the salmon on the griddle and cook until well coloured (about 2 minutes), then carefully turn over.

3. Now turn the heat down and cook on each side until the fish is cooked through. It should take about 4 minutes, but this will depend how thick the steaks are, so keep checking. Arrange on warm plates, with wedges of lime and two slices of the cold butter on top of each steak. Serve with Pineapple, Avocado, Orange and Mint Salad with Ginger Dressing.

I first tasted tilapia in Africa, then it became popular in Brixton market and now it's widely available. It's a great fish with a really firm flesh.

golden tilapia in lime and thyme

Serves 4

4 skinned tilapia fillets (about 450g/ 1lb in total), or other firm white fish such as snapper
juice of 3 limes
2 tbsp plain flour
1 tsp salt
½ tsp pepper
1½ tbsp chopped thyme leaves

sunflower or groundnut oil, for frying
green salad or Caribbean Griddled Aubergine (see page 112), to serve

TO GARNISH
coarse sea salt
1 lime, cut into halves

1. Put the fish in a shallow dish with the lime juice. Cover and let it marinate in the fridge for 30 minutes or up to a couple of hours.

2. Mix the flour with the salt, pepper and thyme. Take the fish out of the lime juice and pat dry with kitchen paper. Dip in the seasoned flour and put to one side.

3. Put enough oil in a large frying pan to lie ½cm (¼in) deep, heat it up well and fry the floured fish fillets for around 2 minutes on each side until just cooked through. It may take slightly longer if the fish fillet is thicker than about 4–5 cm (1½–2in).

4. Sprinkle with coarse sea salt and garnish with lime halves. Serve with a green salad or Caribbean Griddled Aubergine.

Snapper's probably the most widely used of all fish in Caribbean cooking. Here we cook ours in an oven, but if you're planning a beach party, you can cook yours on a barbecue with a lid or a rack set on bricks on a beach fire. Choose a smaller fish than we have here (around 1–2kg/2lb 4oz–4lb 8oz), stuff it, wrap it in foil and cook it over the coals for 35 minutes–1 hour depending on size, turning every 15 minutes or so to ensure it cooks evenly.

hot roast snapper with coconut, chilli and lime salsa

Serves 8

3kg (6lb 8oz) snapper, either pink- or grey-skinned, gutted and scaled
1 lime

FOR THE STUFFING
1 small bunch of fresh coriander, finely chopped
1 small bunch of flat-leaf parsley, finely chopped
leaves from 8 sprigs of thyme
zest of 1 lime
juice of 2 limes
4cm (1½in) piece of root ginger, very finely chopped

1 hot red chilli (ideally Scotch bonnet), deseeded and finely chopped
5-6 tbsp olive oil
salt and pepper

FOR THE SALSA
250g (9oz) fresh coconut flesh
¼ tsp caster sugar
juice of 8 limes
zest of 2 limes
2 red chillies, deseeded and cut into fine slivers
small bunch of fresh coriander, leaves coarsely chopped

1. Preheat the oven to 200°C/400°F/gas mark 6. Using a very sharp knife, make 3 deep slashes on each side of the fish. Squeeze the juice of a lime all over. Mix all the stuffing ingredients together and stuff it into the slits as well as the cavity.

2. Set the fish in a roasting tin lined with foil and roast in the preheated oven, uncovered, for 45 minutes, by which time the flesh closest to the bone at the thickest parts should be perfectly white, not at all 'glassy' looking.

3. To make the salsa use a potato peeler, to make wafer-thin shavings of coconut. Mix the sugar with the lime juice, stirring until it dissolves, and toss the coconut with this and all the other ingredients. Serve with the snapper.

Lily Bolt is the aunt of Jamaican Olympic hero Usain Bolt. His Dad, Wellesley, puts Usain's success down to being brought up on the famous yams of Trelawney, Jamaica. In this recipe, shared with us by Lily, yams are partnered with a fish stew.

fresh brown stew mullet with olympian yams

Serves 2

1 tbsp groundnut or sunflower oil
1 x 500g (1lb 2oz) grey mullet, gutted, scaled and gills removed
large pinch of all-purpose seasoning (or homemade seasoning made up of equal parts ground allspice, ground ginger and grated nutmeg)
1 onion, finely chopped
1 tomato, cut into 1cm (½in) dice
1 spring onion, finely sliced
1 large okra, trimmed and cut into 1cm (½in) slices

1 hot red chilli (ideally Scotch bonnet), deseeded and finely chopped
½ tbsp cider vinegar
1 tbsp soy sauce
1 sprig of thyme
approx. 125g (4½oz) butter or margarine

FOR THE OLYMPIAN YAMS
2 yellow or white yams, about 10cm (4in) long and thick
2 tsp mayonnaise
salt and pepper (optional)

1. Cook the yams either on a barbecue, or in an oven preheated to 200°C/400°F/gas mark 6, for 40–60 minutes, or until tender.

2. Meanwhile, heat the oil in a large heavy-based saucepan that has a lid until medium-hot. Season the fish with the seasoning, place in the saucepan, then fry to brown for around 2 minutes on each side.

3. After frying, turn the heat down to medium-low. Add the chopped vegetables, chilli, vinegar, soy sauce, thyme and butter or margarine to the fish in the saucepan, using more or less of the fat depending on how rich you want the dish to be. Cover the pan and simmer on a moderate heat for 30 minutes.

4. Peel the skin off the yams (or scoop out the flesh) and mix in the mayonnaise. Season if desired. Serve with the fish and sauce.

Try to get clean crab shells from your fishmonger and serve the dish in them for a fantastic effect. This recipe makes an impressive starter, or a light lunch if you add a green salad.

devilled crab gratin

Serves 4

30g (1oz) butter
1 tbsp sunflower or groundnut oil
1 small onion, finely chopped
1 stick of celery, finely chopped
½ red pepper, deseeded and
    cut into 1½cm (⅝in) dice
½ green pepper, deseeded and
    cut into 1½cm (⅝in) dice
1 garlic clove, finely chopped
2 tbsp plain flour
175ml (6fl oz) milk
50ml (2fl oz) double cream
1 tbsp rum
1 tsp West Indian hot sauce, or to taste
2 tsp Dijon mustard
generous squeeze of lemon
salt and pepper
2 tbsp olive oil
250g (9oz) button mushrooms,
    roughly chopped
3 spring onions, green part only,
    finely chopped
600g (1lb 5oz) fresh cooked white
    crab meat

FOR THE TOPPING
30g (1oz) white breadcrumbs
2 tbsp finely chopped flat-leaf parsley
20g (¾oz) grated Parmesan cheese
30g (1oz) melted butter

1. Heat the butter and oil in a heavy-based saucepan and saute the onion, celery and peppers until soft but not coloured. Add the garlic and cook for a further 2 minutes. Now add the flour and stir it round for a minute or so until it is well incorporated. Take the pan off the heat and add the milk little by little, stirring as you do so. Don't add the next bit of milk until the previous amount has been well incorporated or you will end up with a lumpy sauce. Put the pan back on the heat and bring to the boil, stirring constantly. Turn the heat down and cook for 5 minutes, stirring from time to time. Add the cream and rum, the hot sauce, mustard and lemon juice. Taste, season and set aside.

2. Preheat the oven to 200°C/400°F/gas mark 6. Heat the olive oil in a frying pan and sauté the mushrooms until golden, then turn the heat up and drive off the moisture in the pan (mushrooms give out a lot of liquid but you need them to be dry before adding them to the sauce). Add the spring onions and sauté for another couple of minutes, then add the crab and heat it through. Add all of this to the sauce.

3. Gently reheat the sauce and divide between 4 individual gratin dishes or crab shells. Mix the breadcrumbs with the parsley and cheese and sprinkle over the top. Pour over the melted butter and bake in the preheated oven for about 15 minutes, or until golden. Serve immediately.

In the Caribbean, when you catch a big fish such as a grouper, the body can go off to the hotels while the head is used by locals along with some chopped-up vegetables to make what we call 'fish tea' or fish soup. This soup is a special version, using shellfish instead of fish, but you could also use just fish if you prefer.

caribbean seafood soup

Serves 4

2 tbsp sunflower or groundnut oil
1 onion, roughly chopped
1 red pepper, deseeded and finely diced
2 garlic cloves, finely chopped
½ hot red chilli (ideally Scotch bonnet), seeds left in, finely chopped
2cm (¾in) piece of root ginger, finely chopped
½ tsp ground allspice
4 plum tomatoes, roughly chopped
115g (4oz) sweet potato, peeled and cut into small cubes
3 sprigs of fresh thyme
400ml can coconut milk
½ tbsp soft light brown sugar
squeeze of lime
1kg (2lb 4oz) mussels
150g (5½oz) queen (small) scallops, without roe

TO SERVE
zest of 1 lime, cut in thin strips
1 red chilli, deseeded and very finely chopped
fresh coconut shavings

1. Heat the oil in the bottom of a large heavy-based saucepan (it must be able to fit all the mussels) and sauté the onion and pepper until soft. The onion should be pale gold.

2. Add the garlic, chilli, ginger and allspice and cook gently for another 2 minutes. Add the tomatoes and cook for another minute, then add everything else except the shellfish. Bring just up to the boil, then turn down the heat and cook for 15 minutes, or until the sweet potato is tender.

3. Meanwhile, prepare the mussels. Put them into a sink of cold water and remove and discard any 'beards' you can see (these are strands of fibres that attached the mussels to their growing rope). Discard any that have broken shells, or that do not shut tight when tapped on the side of the sink. Rinse and drain well. Rinse the scallops in a sieve with cold water then drain well.

4. Add the mussels and scallops to the pot, cover and cook over a medium heat for 4–5 minutes. In this time the mussels should open and the scallops will poach. Discard any mussels that have not opened.

5. Scatter the lime zest, chilli and coconut shavings over the top, and enjoy!

This really simple supper is made extra-special
if you can find a Scotch bonnet chilli and have
its distinctive taste busting out off the plate.

prawn pasta

Serves 4

100g (3½oz) soft butter, at room
  temperature
1 garlic clove, finely chopped
1 hot red chilli (ideally Scotch bonnet),
  deseeded and thinly sliced
½ tsp salt
12-16 cooked peeled giant prawns,
  or 16-20 cooked peeled king prawns

75-100g (2¾-3½oz) tagliatelle
  for each person
juice and zest of ½ lemon

TO GARNISH
freshly ground black pepper
large handful of chives, finely chopped

1. Mix the butter, garlic, chilli and salt in a bowl. Add the prawns, cover, and leave
in the fridge for at least an hour, if possible.

2. Put a large pan of salted water on to boil. Add the pasta and let it cook in the
boiling water for 8–10 minutes, or until you can feel only a very slight resistance
when you bite into a strand.

3. For the last 4 minutes of pasta cooking time, put the giant prawns with their
flavoured butter in a saucepan and gently heat so the butter melts and the
prawns heat through (king prawns will need only 3 minutes).

4. Toss the cooked tagliatelle with the melted butter and prawns and arrange
on 4 plates. Squeeze over the lemon juice and sprinkle over the zest. Garnish
with black pepper and a sprinkling of chives.

*Levi's tip: Leave the prawns in the garlic butter in the fridge all day
if it's more convenient. They'll just take on even more flavour.*

Christophene (also known as 'cho-cho') is a green, pear-shaped vegetable that is one of my favourites. Seek it out in shops and markets near Caribbean communities. It has a delicate taste that is almost like that of a dense, savoury melon, and a smooth, slippery flesh that holds other flavours very well.

marinade prawns in coconut sauce

Serves 4

½ x quantity Jerk Marinade
   (see page 94)
400g (14oz) cooked peeled North
   Atlantic prawns
1 christophene, or 2 peeled courgettes
½ tbsp sunflower or groundnut oil
1 stick of celery, finely diced

2 shallots, finely diced
200ml (7fl oz) coconut milk
1 bay leaf
juice of about ½ lime, to taste
salt
boiled rice and green salad, to serve

1. Make the jerk marinade, pour it over the prawns and turn them over so they are well coated. Cover and leave in the fridge for at least 4 hours, stirring once or twice.

2. To prepare the christophene, if using, cut it in half, cut out the central pip and peel off the skin. Cut each half into thin slices, as you would an apple. If using courgettes, cut the stalk from each one, cut in half lengthways, then cut into long, medium-thin slices (about ¾cm/⅜in thick and 8cm/3¼in long).

3. Heat the oil in a large saucepan. Over a gentle heat, soften the celery and shallot in the oil. Add the christophene or courgette and cook for a couple of minutes, stirring occasionally, to soften slightly. Add the marinade (but not yet the prawns), coconut milk and bay leaf. Simmer for 15 minutes, until the christophene is tender (only 10 minutes if using courgettes). Add the prawns and cook for 5 minutes, until heated through. Season with a good squeeze or two of lime juice and salt. Caribbean cooks find they don't need to use very much salt with coconut as it has its own sort of saltiness. Serve with rice and salad.

We love curries in the West Indies. This dish is busting out with colour and mixes juicy prawns in a thick, rich tomato sauce with what we call 'Irish potatoes' (as opposed to sweet potatoes). Depending on your tolerance for heat, either chuck all the chilli seeds, keep half, or be brave and put all of them in the sauce: this is meant to be hot! I go for half the seeds for this dish.

hot-hot prawn and potato curry

Serves 4

800g (1lb 12oz) waxy potatoes, such as Desirée, peeled and cut into big chunks
1 tbsp sunflower or groundnut oil
1 onion, finely chopped
1 garlic clove, finely chopped
6cm (2½in) piece of root ginger, finely chopped
2 tsp all-purpose seasoning
1 hot red chilli (ideally Scotch bonnet), finely chopped

½ green pepper, deseeded and cut into thin strips
½ x 420g can chopped tomatoes
300g (10½oz) cooked peeled king prawns
salt
2 tbsp torn fresh coriander leaves, to garnish
boiled rice and green salad, to serve

1. Put the potatoes in a pan of cold water, bring to the boil and simmer for 10 minutes, until part cooked. Drain. Meanwhile, heat the oil in a big saucepan and fry the onion, garlic and ginger over a low heat until soft. Stir in the all-purpose seasoning and cook for a couple of minutes.

2. Add the chilli and as many of its seeds as you dare, along with the pepper. Cook for 5 minutes, stirring occasionally. Add the part-cooked potatoes and the tomatoes. Simmer until the potatoes are cooked through and the sauce is nice and thick (about 10 minutes). Add the prawns and heat through in the sauce (about 3 minutes). Season with salt to taste and garnish with the chopped coriander. Serve with rice and salad.

Roasts & Grills

This makes a knock-out Sunday roast. Thyme, lime, ginger and cinnamon are classic West Indian flavourings. What's unusual is grenadine, normally found in cocktails, used to flavour the meat.

honey, grenadine and ginger roasted lamb with pomegranate and mint salad

Serves 8

3kg (6lb 8oz) leg of lamb
8 tbsp grenadine
10 tbsp runny honey
juice of 3 limes and zest of 2
8 garlic cloves, finely chopped
leaves from 8 sprigs of thyme
2 tsp ground cinnamon
2 tsp ground ginger
salt and pepper

FOR THE SALAD
1 small red onion, very finely sliced
seeds from 2 pomegranates
30g (1oz) mint leaves
2 tbsp lime juice
6 tbsp extra virgin olive oil
salt and pepper

1. Wash the lamb and pat it dry with kitchen paper. Using a small, sharp knife, make incisions all over the meat. Mix all the other ingredients to make a marinade and spread it over the lamb, making sure some goes down into the incisions. Cover with clingfilm and put in the fridge overnight. Turn the lamb over once or twice.

2. Remove the lamb from the fridge and allow it to come to room temperature.

3. Preheat the oven to 220°C/425°F/gas mark 7. Put a sheet of foil big enough to go all around the lamb in a roasting tin, lay the meat on top and season all over. Pull the foil up around the leg to almost cover, leaving it open slightly at the top so steam can escape. Cook the lamb in the preheated oven for 15 minutes, then turn it down to 180°C/350°F/gas mark 4 and cook for a further 2 hours. Open the foil after an hour so that the outside gets a lovely dark glaze, but pull it over again to cover if the honey starts to burn. Baste every so often with the juices and any leftover marinade.

4. When the lamb is cooked through, pull the foil up round it again, cover it with tea towels and leave to rest for 20 minutes before carving. Make the salad just before serving by simply tossing all the ingredients together. Serve the lamb with the cooking juices and the salad.

Levi's tip: To remove the seeds from a pomegranate, cut it in half through its equator then, holding the fruit cut side down over a large bowl, bash it hard with a wooden spoon. The seeds should ricochet out!

A big meal for the family, this is a nice, juicy adventure for everyone to get stuck into. Just look at the cooking time! Did you know you could have roast lamb on the table so quickly? This is really good with Shoestring Sweet Potato Fries (*see* page 116).

butterflied leg of lamb with oregano, thyme, ginger and soy

Serves 8

2.2kg (5lb) leg of lamb, butterfly boned by the butcher
leaves from 4 sprigs of thyme
1 tbsp chopped oregano
grated zest of ½ orange
juice of ½ orange
4 garlic cloves, finely chopped
4 tbsp runny honey

2.5cm (1in) piece of root ginger, grated or finely chopped
1½ tbsp soy sauce
salt and pepper
4 tbsp olive oil
Shoestring Sweet Potato Fries (see page 116), to serve

1. Wash the meat and pat it dry with kitchen paper. Spread it out flat and, with a small, sharp knife, make incisions all over it on both sides. Put it into a large container. Mix all the other ingredients together and spread this marinade all over the lamb. Cover loosely and leave to marinate for at least 2 hours, longer if you can (up to 24 hours), in the fridge. Turn every so often.

2. Take it out of the fridge and allow it to come to room temperature (don't skip this bit, even if you're tempted!). Preheat the oven to 220°C/425°F/gas mark 7.

3. Put the lamb in a roasting tin, fatty side up. Put it into the oven and cook for 15 minutes, then turn the temperature down to 190°C/375°F/gas mark 5 and cook for another 20 minutes (the lamb will be pink). Remove from the oven, cover with foil, insulate with tea towels and leave to rest for 15 minutes.

4. Serve with the cooking juices and Shoestring Sweet Potato Fries.

This dish just looks after itself. Use big, good-quality chops.
As a Rasta I don't eat pork, but here is a recipe for you as it is a
traditional Caribbean ingredient – in fact, the old-school way is
to make jerk pork rather than jerk chicken.

jamaican pork chops

Serves 4

2 tbsp sunflower or groundnut oil
salt and pepper
4 big pork loin chops
1 onion, roughly chopped
1 red pepper, deseeded and cut into
  2cm (¾in) cubes
1 yellow pepper, deseeded and cut into
  2cm (¾in) cubes
2 sticks of celery, cut into 2cm
  (¾in) chunks
2cm (¾in) piece of root ginger,
  finely chopped

2 garlic cloves, finely chopped
4 tbsp brown sugar
3 tsp dry mustard
juice of 1 lime
½ tbsp West Indian hot sauce
3 tbsp tomato purée
400g can tomatoes
150ml (¼ pint) water or chicken stock
  (see page 189)
boiled rice or Rice and Peas
  (see page 120), to serve

1. Preheat the oven to 160°C/325°F/gas mark 3.

2. Wash the meat and pat it dry with kitchen paper. Heat the oil in a frying pan,
season the chops and brown them on both sides. Put them in an ovenproof dish
in which they can lie in a single layer.

3. In the fat left in the pan, cook the onion, peppers and celery until they are quite
soft and the onion is pale gold. Add the ginger and garlic and cook for another
minute, then stir in the sugar, mustard, lime and hot sauce. Cook for another
minute before adding the tomato purée and tomatoes. Season, add the water
or stock, then stir again.

4. Pour this sauce over the chops and cook in the preheated oven for 1½ hours,
or until the pork is tender and cooked through, and the sauce has reduced.
Cover with foil if needed towards the end of cooking if overbrowning.
Serve with rice or Rice and Peas.

Don't be put off by the number of ingredients
in this fantastic rub – it is incredibly simple to
make. Try it on lovely lean venison, other meat
such as chicken breasts, or even some salmon.
This recipe is good with Caribbean Mash
(*see* page 116) or chopped up for a gamey
version of Kickbabs (*see* page 135).

rub-a-dub venison

Serves 4

4 x 130g (4½oz) skinless
   venison steaks
Caribbean Mash, to serve (see page 116)

FOR THE JERK RUB
½ tsp ground allspice
½ tsp ground ginger

½ tsp pepper
½ tsp chilli powder
1 garlic clove, finely chopped
leaves from 2 sprigs of thyme
1 tsp salt
1 tbsp sunflower or groundnut oil

1. Wash the venison steaks and pat them dry with kitchen paper. Mix the jerk rub
ingredients together and rub all over the steaks. Leave the meat, covered, in the
fridge for a couple of hours or even overnight to pick up more flavour.

2. Preheat the oven to 220°C/425°F/gas mark 7. Put a shallow baking sheet in the
oven to get it nice and hot. Put the meat on the sheet and cook in the preheated
oven for 6–8 minutes, depending on whether you like your meat with some pink
or done-through but still juicy, turning over halfway.

3. Remove the meat from the oven, cover with foil and leave to rest for a minute
or two, to allow the juices to redistribute through the meat.

4. Cut the steak into thick slices. Serve on a bed of Caribbean Mash and drizzle
with the steak juices.

This recipe comes from Beverley Forbes, owner and cook of Plantation restaurant in Cotham, Bristol. Serve it with Rice and Peas (see page 120) or Caribbean Mash (see page 116).

steak, peppers and tomatoes with ackee and mushrooms

Serves 4

½ tsp sunflower or groundnut oil, plus 1 tsp for rubbing into the steak
8 x 125g (4½oz) pieces of fillet steak
1 onion, finely sliced
125g (4½oz) mixed peppers, deseeded and cut into thin strips
3 sprigs of thyme
1 garlic clove, finely chopped
2 tsp dark soy sauce
3 tsp tomato purée
4 tomatoes, roughly chopped
300ml (½ pint) hot water
salt and pepper

FOR THE ACKEE AND MUSHROOMS
2 tbsp sunflower or groundnut oil
½ onion, finely sliced
½ red pepper, deseeded and cut into thin strips
½ yellow pepper, deseeded and cut into thin strips
½ green pepper, deseeded and cut into thin strips
1 large tomato, finely chopped
250g (9oz) mushrooms, chopped
approx. 150ml (¼ pint) hot water
salt and pepper
347g can ackee, drained
1 spring onion, finely chopped

1. Start with the ackee. Heat the oil in a heavy-based saucepan and cook the onion and peppers over a medium heat until soft, stirring often. Add the tomato and cook for 1–2 minutes, stirring occasionally. Stir in the mushrooms and cook for a few minutes more, letting the natural juices come through and evaporate. Then add as much of the water as you'd like to create a bit more sauce. Season with salt and pepper. Very carefully fold in the ackee. Simmer for 2–3 minutes until heated through. Garnish with spring onion. Keep warm until ready to serve.

2. To cook the steak, heat a heavy-based frying pan until hot. Rub the oil on both sides of the steak. Place the steak in the hot frying pan and brown. Cook to your preference – 1½–2 minutes on each side for medium rare, slightly less for rare and longer for well done. Set aside.

3. Meanwhile, heat the ½ tsp oil in a separate heavy-based saucepan and cook the onion and peppers over a medium heat, stirring often, until soft. Add the rest of the ingredients except for the salt and pepper, mix well and continue to cook, stirring occasionally, until all the vegetables are almost cooked (about 5 minutes). Season with salt and pepper, to taste, bearing in mind the soy sauce is already salty. Place the cooked steak in the sauce and cook until heated through.

4. Serve the steak in its pepper and tomato sauce accompanied by the ackee and mushrooms.

The French-Caribbean phrase, 'C'est chien', means, 'It's delicious', and this sauce is hot, wonderful and very simple. Great with fish and barbecue chicken, too.

griddled steak with sauce chien

Serves 4

4 x 300-400g (10½-14oz) thick
  fillet steaks
sunflower or groundnut oil
salt and pepper

FOR THE SAUCE CHIEN
juice of 4 limes
2 tbsp mild olive oil

3 tbsp roughly chopped flat-leaf
  parsley
4 garlic cloves, finely chopped
½ hot red chilli (ideally Scotch bonnet),
  seeds left in, chopped
6 spring onions, green part only,
  finely chopped

1. Mix everything for the sauce together and pour over 50ml (2fl oz) boiling water. Leave to cool and infuse. That's your sauce!

2. Wash the steaks and pat them dry with kitchen paper. Heat a griddle until very hot. Brush the steaks on each side with oil and season them all over. Slap them on to the griddle pan and cook over a high heat for 1 minute on each side to get a good colour, but don't move the steaks until they are easy to turn over or you might tear the flesh.

3. Turn the heat down to medium and continue to cook until the meat is done to your liking. It should take 3–4 minutes more in total (make sure you turn them at least once during this time) for rare to medium-rare steaks. Serve with the delicious sauce on the side.

Poussins are young chickens. In Jamaica we kept chickens and, when friends came round, we would go and fetch the youngest chicken to make a meal. I used to look after the birds and my grandfather taught me how to kill them. You learn so many lessons in life when you live as naturally as we did. As a boy I was learning all about farming and how to get the best out of food. Spatchcocked simply means that the backbone has been removed and the bird splayed out for easier cooking. Buy your poussins already spatchcocked from supermarkets, or get the butcher to do them for you.

spatchcocked poussins with rum barbecue sauce

Serves 4

juice of 1 lime
4 spatchcocked poussins
sunflower or groundnut oil
salt and pepper

FOR THE SAUCE
2 tbsp sunflower or groundnut oil
1 onion, finely chopped
2 garlic cloves, finely chopped
2cm (¾in) piece of root ginger,
    finely chopped
1 tbsp allspice berries, crushed
½ red chilli, deseeded and
    finely chopped
80ml (2½fl oz) tomato ketchup
227g can tomatoes
85g (3oz) molasses sugar
40g (1½oz) light brown sugar
150ml (¼ pint) white wine or
    cider vinegar
150ml (¼ pint) dark rum

1. Squeeze the lime over the poussins and leave, covered, for about 30 minutes.

2. Heat the oil for the sauce in a heavy-based saucepan and add the onion, garlic and ginger. Cook over a medium heat for about 7 minutes, stirring a little, until the onions are soft but not coloured. Add the allspice and cook for another minute. Now add all the other ingredients and bring to the boil, stirring to help the sugar melt. Reduce the heat and simmer gently for 20 minutes.

3. Brush the poussins with oil and season all over. Heat a griddle pan until very hot and add the birds, turning until they are a good colour on both sides. Then reduce the heat and continue to cook until almost ready and the juices run clear when a skewer is pushed into the thickest point – they should take about 8 minutes on each side.

4. When the poussins are almost ready, paint or spoon the barbecue sauce on to each side, then fry again on each side for another couple of minutes.

Pile these chicken wings high and serve them hot, hot, hot! The marinade is adapted from one by Bob Marley's chef, Gilly. In the late 1970s when Bob was in London, I played football with him and lots of other Rastas in Battersea Park at weekends. Gilly would always have food prepared for afterwards and this jerk marinade is inspired by what he made for us. I love the sugared oranges with these but they also work as a refreshing pudding. You could use blood oranges as an alternative if they're in season and you can find them.

sticky jerk wings with sugared oranges

Serves 4 as a starter or as part of a barbecue spread

12 chicken wings
2 tbsp soft light brown or
  demerara sugar
2 pipless oranges
5 long, mild red chillies, whole
  and undamaged

FOR THE JERK MARINADE
4 spring onions, green part only,
  roughly chopped
1 hot red chilli (ideally Scotch bonnet),
  seeds left in
3cm (1¼in) piece of root ginger,
  cut into chunks
2 tbsp thyme leaves
100ml (3½fl oz) cider vinegar
3 tbsp honey
2 tsp ground allspice
1 tsp ground cinnamon
2 tbsp olive oil
salt and pepper

1. Put the marinade ingredients in a blender and whizz until smooth. Alternately, pound the ingredients to a paste using a pestle and mortar. Pour it over the wings, turning them over so they are well coated. Leave to marinate, covered, in the fridge for at least 4 hours, or overnight if more convenient, turning the wings over once or twice.

2. Get a barbecue going until the coals die down to hot grey ash (or preheat an oven to 190°C/375°F/gas mark 5). Barbecue or cook the wings, turning them over a few times, until they are cooked through (the juices should run clear when a skewer is pushed into the thickest point) and nicely brown, basting with any leftover jerk marinade (about 15 minutes).

3. While the wings are cooking, sprinkle the sugar on to a plate and cut the oranges into quarters. Dip the cut sides of each piece into the sugar and cook on the barbecue (or in a heavy dry frying pan or under a stovetop grill) for a few minutes until the sugar has caramelized. Keep a close eye on the oranges to prevent them from burning. At the same time, chargrill the chillies.

4. Serve the wings with the caramelized oranges and chargrilled chillies.

If you like cooking with fire you'll love this. There's nothing cooler than taking something flambéed to the table – it's real theatre. This is what I cook for Christmas. Use ordinary bananas rather than plantain inside or alongside the bird if you prefer, or if you can't get hold of plantain. This is definitely one to wow friends with at Sunday lunch.

haitian roast chicken with two stuffings

Serves 6

1.6kg (3½lb) roasting chicken
30g (1oz) butter
2 very ripe plantains, peeled
    and sliced
2 plum tomatoes, quartered
salt and pepper
2 tsp cayenne pepper
350ml (12fl oz) chicken stock
    (see page 189)
4 tbsp rum

FOR THE BREAD STUFFING
50g (1¾oz) butter
½ onion, finely chopped
2 spring onions, chopped
2 garlic cloves, finely chopped
generous grating of nutmeg
3 slices of white bread, made
    into breadcrumbs
leaves from 4 sprigs of thyme
zest and juice of 1 lime
2 tbsp rum
2 tsp soft light brown or
    demerara sugar

1. For the bread stuffing, melt the butter in a frying pan and cook the onion until soft. Add the spring onions and garlic and cook for 2 minutes more. Add the nutmeg and breadcrumbs; cook until golden. Add the thyme, lime zest and juice, rum and sugar. Starting from the loose skin at the neck end, ease the skin from the breast meat of the bird with your fingers – do this very gently as you don't want to remove the skin or tear it – reaching as far as you can down the legs and stopping before you reach the end of each breast. Push the stuffing under the skin of the bird then tuck the neck skin back underneath.

2. Preheat the oven to 190°C/375°F/gas mark 5. Melt half the butter in a frying pan and fry the plantain until cooked. Add the tomatoes, soften slightly and season. You can stuff the bird with this mixture, or make it while the bird is cooking and roast it alongside the bird for the last half-hour of cooking time. Smear the remaining butter over the bird and season with cayenne, salt and pepper. Set in a roasting tin and roast in the oven for 1½ hours (1¾ hours if stuffed). Push a skewer into the thigh at the thickest point. If the juices run clear, it is done; if not, give it another 5 minutes, then test again.

3. Put the bird on a heated platter and cover with foil. Add the chicken stock to the juices in the tin, scraping up the brown bits from the bottom. Boil this until you have a liquid with a gravy-like consistency, then pour through a sieve into a warm gravy boat. Put the plantain mixture around the bird. Heat the rum in a frying pan and set it alight. Pour over the bird and carry it proudly to the table. Serve the chicken with the gravy.

When I was growing up, we'd never use tamarind in cooking. We'd just pick it off the tree and eat it. This recipe draws from the experience I've picked up more recently, and I can hear my grandmother saying to me, 'Go on my son, this is what you've learned: well done.' This recipe is gorgeously sweet and sour and really makes your mouth pucker. You could try the same flavourings with pork chops. Eat this with plain boiled rice and green salad, or try it with Pineapple, Avocado, Orange and Mint Salad with Ginger Dressing (*see* page 107).

tamarind and molasses roast chicken

Serves 4

3½ tbsp tamarind paste
2 tbsp runny honey
2½ tbsp molasses sugar
2 garlic cloves, finely chopped

8 chicken thighs or mixture of thighs
 and drumsticks
rice and green salad, to serve

1. Mix together the tamarind paste, honey, sugar and garlic, then stir until you have a really smooth paste. Paint or spoon it all over the chicken. If you have time, leave it to marinate, covered with clingfilm, in the fridge for anything from 1 hour to overnight, turning over every so often.

2. Preheat the oven to 180°C/350°F/gas mark 4. Put the marinated chicken in a roasting dish and roast in the preheated oven for 30–40 minutes. Check that the chicken is cooked through (pierce the thickest piece of chicken with a skewer – if the juices run clear, it is done; if not, give it another 5 minutes, then test again). Serve with rice and green salad.

Children love this dish, which is inspired by the beautiful, sun-fresh island of Antigua. It is great with fresh pineapple but you could use canned in natural juice.

antiguan chicken with pineapple

Serves 4

juice and finely grated zest of 1 lime
8 chicken pieces
salt and pepper
2 tbsp sunflower or groundnut oil
1 onion, roughly chopped
1 garlic clove, finely chopped
2 tomatoes, coarsely chopped
1 red chilli, deseeded and
   finely chopped

5 tbsp raisins
6 sprigs of fresh thyme
2 bay leaves
300ml (½ pint) chicken stock
   (see page 189)
350g (12oz) chopped pineapple
4 tbsp rum (optional)
boiled rice, to serve

1. Rub the lime juice and zest all over the chicken and season. Cover with clingfilm and leave in the fridge for 30 minutes.

2. Heat the oil in a casserole and fry the chicken all over until it is a lovely golden colour. Take out of the pan and set aside.

3. In the same pan, sauté the onion and garlic until they are pale gold, then add the tomatoes, chilli, raisins, thyme and bay and cook for 5 minutes.

4. Return the chicken and add enough stock to cover. Bring up to the boil, then turn down to a simmer and partially cover the pan. Cook for 35 minutes, or until the chicken is cooked through (pierce the thickest piece of chicken with a skewer – if the juices run clear, it is done; if not, give it another 5 minutes, then test again). The juices will evaporate a little, making a thickish sauce.

5. Add the pineapple, plus any juice that came out when you chopped it, to the chicken and cook gently until soft and a bit mushy – about 10 minutes. Add the rum, if using, and cook for another 5 minutes. This is lovely with rice.

On the Side

When I first came across this dish it was a salsa, eaten as an accompaniment to grilled meat and fish. Then I chopped it all up differently and turned it into a colourful salad. Eat on its own as a starter or serve alongside simply cooked chicken, pork, fish, prawns or baked sweet potato.

avocado and mango salad

Serves 4

2 avocados
1 just-ripe (but still firm) mango
2 little gem lettuces, separated into
   leaves, washed and dried
½ long, mild red chilli, deseeded and
   chopped into slivers

½ red onion, thinly sliced
2 sprigs of thyme, leaves only
juice of 1 lime
olive oil
salt

1. Cut the avocados in half, remove the stones, peel and cut the flesh into long thin slices. Cut both cheeks from the mango stone and cross-hatch the flesh, making sure your knife goes right down to the skin but not through it. Press the centre of each piece of the mango skin with your fingers so that the straight, cut flesh side becomes rounded (it will look like a mango hedgehog), then use the knife to disconnect the squares of mango: you will have cubes of mango. Remove any remaining mango flesh that you can reach, peel and dice it and add to the rest.

2. Put the lettuce leaves on to 4 plates. Arrange the avocado, mango, chilli and onion on top. Sprinkle over the thyme leaves, squeeze over the lime and drizzle over some olive oil. Season with salt.

Levi's tip: To make this recipe as a salsa, chop the avocados, mango, chilli and onion finely. Sprinkle over the thyme leaves, squeeze over the lime, drizzle over some olive oil, then season with salt. Mix with cooked white crab meat, if you like. Spoon the salsa into individual little gem lettuce leaves and serve.

This Caribbean take on an Italian classic has got the Jamaican and Rasta colours of green, gold and red. It's a great dish for a barbecue or to have as part of an all-good-and-ready-done summer lunch or supper.

green, gold and red pepper salad

Serves 4–5

2 green peppers, skinned
2 red peppers, skinned
2 yellow peppers, skinned
3 tbsp olive oil

1 tsp demerara sugar
zest of ½ lime
salt
2 tbsp chopped fresh coriander leaves

1. Heat a grill to its highest setting. Cut all the peppers in half, then cut out and discard the stalks and seeds. Grill until the skin is charred all over, moving them once or twice to get them to blacken all over. (You can also cook them on the barbecue if you've got it going.) Put the peppers in a plastic bag and leave them to cool for 10 minutes.

2. Peel the peppers (discard the skin) and slice them into long, finger-thick strips. Put them and any of their delicious juices into a serving bowl.

3. Whisk the sugar and lime zest into the 3 tbsp olive oil and season with salt to taste. Stir the dressing into the peppers with the coriander leaves. Check the seasoning.

4. Ideally, serve this salad at room temperature – you can leave it covered on the side of the kitchen for a couple of hours. If making the day before, keep it covered in the fridge but make sure you bring it to room temperature before serving.

Here's a dish for summertime, full of sunshine fun. It's one to take into the garden with your loved ones and enjoy for its colours and the great burst of freshness from the mint. It is also lovely if you leave out the orange and add prawns or cooked white crab meat. Don't be tempted to add salad leaves though; it is better like this.

pineapple, avocado, orange and mint salad with ginger dressing

Serves 6 as a side dish

1 small juicy pineapple
2 avocados
2 oranges
30g (1oz) mint leaves, torn

FOR THE DRESSING
juice of 1 lime

salt and pepper
2 tbsp olive oil
½ knob of preserved stem ginger, finely chopped
1 tbsp syrup from jar of preserved stem ginger

1. To make the dressing, simply whisk everything together.

2. Cut the skin from the pineapple and halve the fruit. Cut into slices about 1cm (½in) thick and remove and discard the tough core that goes right through the centre. Chop it into smaller pieces as shown, if you like.

3. Halve, stone and peel the avocados and slice each half.

4. Cut the top and bottom from each orange so that it can sit on a flat base. Now cut the rind off with a small, sharp knife, working from top to bottom, all round the fruit, making sure you remove all the bitter white pith. Break the oranges into segments, flicking out any seeds with the point of a sharp knife.

5. Arrange the fruit on a serving plate, placing a small pile of the torn mint leaves in the centre. Season. (I know there's seasoning in the dressing but somehow avocado is always better seasoned directly on to the flesh.) Now dress the salad and serve immediately.

My daughter Shar makes the best coleslaw ever and this is her fantastic recipe. It is full of colour, flavour and crunch and doesn't have too much sauce – just how I like it.

shar's coleslaw

Serves 4–6

¼ firm white cabbage (about 300g/10½oz), very finely sliced
⅛ red cabbage (about 160g/5¾oz), very finely sliced
125g (4½oz) carrots, grated
½ green pepper, deseeded and finely diced
2 spring onions, green part only, finely diced

175g (6oz) canned sweetcorn, drained
2 tbsp finely chopped fresh coriander leaves
salt and pepper
juice of ½ lime
1 tbsp mayonnaise

1. Mix all the prepared vegetables with the sweetcorn and coriander in a serving bowl. Season, then squeeze on the lime and dollop on the mayo. Stir everything together carefully. That's it: fresh and fantastic.

2. Keep the coleslaw, covered, in the fridge if you're preparing it in advance of the meal. This is great at a barbecue or any summer meal, or even to make you feel like being healthy in winter.

This is good with fried chicken or a slice of ham, or as a light supper or lunch with a tomato salad. Okra, also known as ladies' fingers, is a taste you grow into. I've never known a child who likes them, because of their slimy texture, and I've never known an adult who doesn't! The trick is to pile up the cheese; when it melts it is nice and crisp on top. You could also vary the recipe by using another cheese, such as Red Leicester or Gruyère.

okra with green beans

Serves 4 as a starter or side dish

32 medium okra (about 200g/7oz)
200g (7oz) green beans, topped
15g (½oz) butter
2 tbsp water
2 tbsp cider vinegar
salt and pepper
100g (3½oz) Cheddar cheese, grated
4 tbsp chopped fresh coriander
    leaves, to garnish (optional)

1. Preheat the oven to 180°C/350°F/gas mark 4. Trim the ends from the okra.

2. Put a pan of salted water on to boil. When boiling, plunge in the beans for 3 minutes, then drain.

3. Meanwhile, melt the butter in a saucepan and add the okra. Stir around for a couple of minutes over a medium heat then add the water and cider vinegar. Cover with a lid and let them steam over a low heat, stirring once or twice, for 2 minutes, then season.

4. Layer up the okra and beans in 4 individual heatproof dishes, starting with a layer of half the okra (4 in a dish), followed by half the beans, set on top at right angles to the okra. Repeat with the rest of the ingredients so you have 4 layers in all.

5. Sprinkle over the cheese, finish with a grinding of pepper and put in the oven for 10 minutes, or until the cheese is melting and bubbly. Serve immediately, sprinkled with coriander leaves, if liked.

With lots of vegetables and good fresh cooking, this is very Rasta, very natural, very ital – or as we say, vital! It's incredibly versatile – serve as a starter on its own, or with baked potatoes for a main course, or alongside meat or fish.

caribbean griddled aubergine

Serves 4

5 tbsp olive oil, plus 2 tbsp to brush on aubergines

3 yellow peppers, deseeded and finely diced

3 sticks of celery, finely diced

125g (4½oz) butternut squash, peeled, deseeded and finely diced

3 garlic cloves, finely chopped

2 large aubergines, cut into rounds 1-1½cm (½-⅝in) thick

½-1½ hot red chilli (ideally Scotch bonnet), deseeded and finely chopped, to taste

3 tbsp tomato purée

3 tbsp tamarind paste

2 tbsp demerara sugar, to taste

2 tbsp fresh coriander or flat-leaf parsley leaves, to garnish

1. Preheat the oven to 180°C/350°F/gas mark 4.

2. Heat the oil in a large saucepan and add the peppers, celery, butternut squash and garlic, cooking until almost soft (about 10 minutes). Meanwhile, brush the aubergines with oil and fry very quickly in another pan, on both sides, to brown (this looks great done on a ridged griddle, or you can use a frying pan).

3. Add the chilli, tomato puree, tamarind and sugar (go carefully with the sugar) to the softening diced vegetables along with 4–5 tbsp water and cook for another 5 minutes. Taste, and add more sugar or tamarind if necessary to get a good sweet and sour balance.

4. Put the aubergines in an ovenproof dish. Top with dollops of the sauce and cover (use foil if you don't have a lid). Cook in the oven for 20–25 minutes, or until the aubergine is tender. Serve garnished with coriander or parsley leaves.

Sweet potato wedges are like Jamaican fries. You get them in the patty shops, where you can buy a nice juicy patty, a bagful of wedges and a refreshing glass of lime wash (*see* Caribbean Wash, page 187). These are lovely on their own or great with the jerk butter melting over the top. The jerk butter is also great served melting over fish or chicken.

hot sweet potato wedges with jerk butter

Serves 8 as a side dish

1.4kg (3lb 3½oz) sweet potatoes, peeled and sliced about the size of an orange segment
5 tbsp sunflower or groundnut oil
3 tbsp soft light brown sugar
juice of 2 limes
pepper

FOR THE JERK BUTTER
50g (1¾oz) butter, slightly softened
½ tbsp ground allspice
½ tsp ground ginger
½ tsp cayenne
½ tbsp black peppercorns, ground
½ tsp cinnamon, ground
leaves from 2 sprigs of thyme
2 garlic cloves, finely chopped
generous grating of fresh nutmeg
2 tsp brown sugar
salt
juice of ½ lime

1. Preheat the oven to 200°C/400°F/gas mark 6. Mix the sweet potato slices with the olive oil, brown sugar and lime juice and season with pepper, turning them over in the flavourings with your hands. Lay them in a roasting tin in which the slices can lie in a single layer. Put into the oven and roast until tender – about 20 minutes – turning over halfway through.

2. Meanwhile, make the butter by mashing everything together. Either chill to let cold pats melt over the wedges, or use it already melted as a dip.

These are great with Lime, Chilli and Coriander Mayo (*see* page 126).

shoestring sweet potato fries

Serves 4

2 large sweet potatoes, peeled
sunflower or groundnut oil for
   deep-frying
1 hot red chilli (ideally Scotch bonnet),
   whole and undamaged
2 garlic cloves, peeled
flaked sea salt

1. Cut the sweet potatoes into strips the size of very skinny fries (the same length but half the thickness of fast-food fries).

2. Half fill a large pan with oil and put it over a moderate heat, heating until the oil temperature on a cook's thermometer is 190°C/375°F. It needs to be this hot so the fries crisp up rather than soggily soaking up oil, as they will at lower temperatures. You don't need me to tell you to be very careful with a pan of hot oil, and don't leave it unattended.

3. Add the sweet potatoes to the oil, along with the chilli and garlic, which will gently flavour the oil. Deep-fry until tender and dark gold – about 10 minutes – then remove with a slotted spoon. Drain immediately on kitchen paper and salt well. Crunch and enjoy!

A dubbed-up version of a British classic, this is great with some fried chicken, or used as the sunny-orange topping for my Caribbean Fish Pie (*see* page 62).

caribbean mash

Serves 4

900g (2lb) sweet potatoes, peeled
40g (1½oz) butter
good grating of nutmeg
pinch of ground allspice
salt and pepper

1. Cut the potatoes into medium, equal-sized chunks. Put in cold water, bring to the boil and simmer until tender (it's faster than ordinary potatoes; only about 8–10 minutes).

2. Mash with the butter and season with nutmeg, allspice and salt and pepper, to taste.

Ripe plantain should be patched with black on the outside. The pale, orange-gold fruit inside tastes of banana, pineapple and cucumber.

saucy plantain

Serves 2 (makes about 5 pieces)

½ ripe plantain, peeled
1 tbsp Banana Sauce (*see below*)
sunflower or groundnut oil, for frying

TO SERVE
sea salt
lime juice
lime wedges

1. Cut each plantain in half down the middle, then cut each half into long slices about 1–1½cm (generous ½in) thick. Put into a dish, add the sauce and turn the plantain over, piercing each piece with a fork to help flavour. Leave for an hour or two, if you can, but cook straight away if you haven't the time.

2. Heat 1cm (½in) of oil in a large frying pan for a minute or two over a medium heat, then fry the plantain pieces for 2–3 minutes each side, turning once, until brown and sticky. Drain on kitchen paper and keep warm in a low oven while you finish the job. Just before serving, sprinkle with sea salt and squeeze over a bit of lime. Serve with lime wedges.

You can spread this on anything and eat it like a jam or a sauce.

banana sauce

Makes about 450ml (16fl oz)

227g can tomatoes
3 ripe bananas, peeled and sliced
3cm (1¼in) piece of root ginger, chopped
¼ garlic clove, finely chopped
2 spring onions, green part only, chopped
1 hot chilli, deseeded and chopped
good grating of nutmeg
leaves from 2 sprigs of thyme
¾ tsp ground allspice
¾ tsp ground cinnamon
2½ tbsp dark soft brown sugar
really generous pinch of salt
juice of 1 lime

1. All you have to do is put everything in a blender and whizz it until smooth, pushing down the gubbins from the sides once or twice. Check the taste and adjust the sugar, salt and lime as necessary to get the right balance.

2. Put into a saucepan and simmer for 5 minutes. Taste again and adjust the seasoning if needed. Cool and keep, covered, in the fridge for up to 4 days.

This is the first dish people mention when they think of Jamaican food. It's a classic. It is important to get a well-flavoured base to cook the rice in. This is called the 'soup', as you should almost be able to drink it on its own. Be careful to use a Scotch bonnet chilli that is completely undamaged. One tiny hole and the seeds will spill out and make your Rice and Peas blisteringly hot, so watch it!

rice and peas (black bean style)

Serves 6

1 fresh coconut
850ml (1½ pint) warm water
1 hot red chilli (ideally Scotch bonnet), whole and undamaged
7 allspice berries
2 sprigs of thyme
1 garlic clove, peeled
1 spring onion, bruised with a rolling pin
½ onion, roughly chopped 400g can
30g (1oz) butter
black beans, drained
salt and pepper
450g (1lb) basmati rice

1. First you need to get into your coconut. Decide which of the three 'eyes' (you'll see them at one end) is the one you are most likely to be able to break into – only one will work! Try to penetrate it with a strong, sharp-tipped knife. If that one doesn't work, try the others. Pour the coconut water out through the hole and set aside. Smash the coconut (doing this outside against a bit of concrete is a good idea). Using a small, sharp knife, lever the coconut flesh away from the shell.

2. Grate the coconut into a bowl. Pour 650ml (1 pint 2fl oz) water over and stir. Lift the coconut flesh up in fistfuls and squeeze out all the juice into the water. Put the squeezed clumps of grated coconut into a sieve, transfer the coconut water to a saucepan, tip the squeezed coconut back into the bowl and cover with the remaining water. Again lift the coconut flesh up in fistfuls and squeeze out all the juice into the water. Transfer the coconut water to the saucepan. Discard the squeezed-out flesh. Add the coconut water from the coconut to the saucepan at this stage, if you like. Add all the remaining ingredients, except the basmati, to the saucepan. Bring to the boil, cover, then turn down and simmer over a medium heat for 15 minutes.

3. Meanwhile, wash the rice, in cold running water until the water is almost clear. Drain, then add to the coconut base. You may need to add some water to bring the level to about 2½cm (1in) above the level of the rice. Season again. Bring to the boil, then cover the rice immediately. Turn the heat down to its lowest level and cook for 15–20 minutes – don't stir it, and don't peek inside! Fish out the spring onion, thyme and chilli, give it a fork to stir it up, and serve immediately.

This brightly coloured rice looks and tastes beautiful with the Caribbean Lamb Shanks (*see* page 18). We have a riddle that goes: 'How water walk to ah pumpkin belly?' The answer is the long vine that leads to the pumpkin.

pumpkin rice

Serves 8–9

550ml (just under a pint) water
400g (14oz) pumpkin, peeled,
  deseeded and cut into small chunks
2-3 sprigs of thyme

1 tsp salt
450g (1lb) basmati rice
15g (½oz) butter

1. Put the water, pumpkin, 2 sprigs of thyme and salt in a saucepan. Put on a lid. Bring to the boil, turn down the heat and simmer, covered, for 10 minutes or until soft. Remove the thyme and very roughly mash the pumpkin into the liquid with a potato masher. You are not after a smooth purée, more a rough mix.

2. Wash the rice twice to remove some of the starch, swishing it round a bowl and running cold water over it until the water is almost clear, and add it to the pumpkin mix in the saucepan. You want the liquid to cover the rice by about 2½cm (1in). Add a little more water if necessary (or pour off some if there's too much). Add the butter and stir it in as it melts. Put the lid back on the pan. Bring to the boil and turn down to a simmer immediately.

3. Leave to simmer gently for around 20 minutes. Do not uncover the pan to take a peek as you want to keep in the heat. The bottom of the rice will brown a little; this is how it is meant to be. Just make sure it is on the lowest heat and, if you have a heat diffuser, you could put it under the pan as well. Turn off the heat and leave for a few more minutes, or until you're ready to eat. Add the remaining sprig of thyme and, if you want to serve it with lots of style, pack into a lightly oiled dish and turn it out in a neat mound on to a serving plate.

This is my version of Caribbean 'coco breads'. These don't contain coconut so the name is a mystery – perhaps they got it because you split each open, like a coconut, then stuff a filling inside. When I first made them, they were more loco than coco, but very good all the same. They've got two pockets you can fill with anything you want. I like to put grated cheese and salad on one side and Chicken Kickbabs (*see* page 135) or fried veggies on the other. But you could use anything. The world is your loco bread!

loco breads

Makes 8

450g (1lb) strong white flour,
   plus extra for dusting
1 tsp caster sugar
1 tsp salt
7g packet fast-action dried yeast
175ml (6fl oz) milk
50ml (2fl oz) water
1 lightly beaten egg
100g (3½oz) butter

1. In a big bowl, mix together the flour, sugar, salt and yeast. Heat the milk and water together until just warm. Stir in the egg. Pour the liquid into the dry ingredients and stir first with a table knife, then with your hands, until you've got a dough. Knead this on a floured work surface for 5–10 minutes, until firm and smooth. Put into a clean bowl, cover with a tea towel and leave in a warm place for an hour to rise.

2. Preheat the oven to 220°C/425°F/gas mark 7. Put a large shallow baking tray on the top shelf and put a deep baking tray filled with water on the bottom. Melt the butter in a small saucepan. Cut the dough into 8 pieces.

3. On a floured work surface, roll out a piece of dough into a circle about 24cm (9½in) in diameter. Brush with melted butter and fold it in half to get a semi-circle. Give it a quick roll, keeping the same shape, and take care to pinch the edges together well. Brush the semicircle with more butter and fold in half once more to get a quarter circle. You will have four layers of bread. Pinch the two central layers together firmly so they are sealed together at the wide top and down the sides. You should now have a cone-shaped bread with two pockets in the middle. Repeat with all eight pieces of dough.

4. Put the breads on the hot tray in the preheated oven and cook for 10–15 minutes, or until nice and brown – a bit like a coconut, or a loconut!

Sauce-making is so easy done this way! This spice-fragrant,
natural ketchup is delicious in Chicken Kickbabs (*see* page 135)
or with meat, or baked potatoes – or chips, of course.

my special tomato sauce

Serves 4

400g can tomatoes
3cm (1¼in) piece of root ginger,
   chopped
¼ garlic clove, finely chopped
2 spring onions, green part only,
   chopped
1 hot red chilli (ideally Scotch bonnet),
   deseeded and chopped
good grating of nutmeg
   (about a whole nutmeg)
leaves from 2 sprigs of thyme
¾ tsp ground allspice
¾ tsp ground cinnamon
2 tbsp demerara sugar, to taste
1 tsp salt
juice of ½–1 lime, to taste

1. All you have to do is put everything in a blender and whizz
it until smooth, pushing down the gubbins from the sides of
the blender once or twice.

2. Check the taste and adjust the sugar, salt and lime to get
the balance you want.

3. Put into a saucepan and simmer for 5 minutes. Taste again
and adjust the seasoning if needed. Keep the sauce, covered,
in the fridge – it will be good for about a week.

Instead of using ready-made mayonnaise, why not make this spicy Caribbean version of it yourself to impress your friends?

lime, chilli and coriander mayo

Serves 6–8

2 egg yolks
1 tsp Dijon mustard
salt and pepper
1 fat garlic clove, finely chopped
juice of 1 lime
290ml (9¾fl oz) sunflower,
   groundnut or light olive oil
1 red chilli, deseeded (keep half
   the seeds) and shredded
leaves from a small bunch of fresh
   coriander, very finely chopped

1. Put the egg yolks into a bowl and mix with the mustard, seasoning, garlic and a little of the lime juice (you probably won't need it all). Using an electric hand beater or a wooden spoon, beat the yolk mixture and gradually start to add the oil, a drop at a time. Keep going – the mixture will really thicken – until it's all in. If it looks as though it might split, add a spoonful or so of warm water and stir it in. This usually 'brings it back'.

2. If you find your mayonnaise is too thick, add a little more warm water until you get it the way you like it.

3. Stir in the chilli, including half the seeds, the coriander and more lime juice to taste.

I love the refreshing aroma and flavour of mint and it goes perfectly with pineapple and juicy spring onions.

pineapple and mint salsa

Serves 4

1 small pineapple
1 red chilli, deseeded and very
   finely sliced
2 spring onions, green part only,
   finely chopped
4 tbsp chopped mint leaves
juice of 1 lime
2 tbsp olive oil
1½ tsp caster sugar

1. Peel the pineapple and cut it into quarters from top to bottom. Remove and discard the hard core. Cut the flesh into small chunks.

2. Mix with all the other ingredients and leave it, covered, for about an hour (but not longer than 90 minutes) for the flavours to meld.

Here's a Caribbean version of a classic Italian sauce that is magic with a seafood barbecue (*see* pages 144–7) or try it with grilled fish, chicken or vegetables.

caribbean salsa verde

Serves 6–8

small bunch of fresh coriander
  (75g/2½oz)
leaves from 5 sprigs of tarragon
10 big basil leaves
½ garlic clove, finely chopped (optional)
2 tsp capers, drained and
  finely chopped
grated zest of ¾ lime

3 anchovy fillets in oil, drained and
  finely chopped
½ green chilli, deseeded and
  finely chopped
juice of ½ lime
5–6 tbsp olive oil
salt, to taste

1. Remove the leaves from the coriander. Finely chop the stalks. Chop the coriander leaves with the tarragon and basil. Put into a bowl with the chopped coriander stalks.

2. Stir the other ingredients into the sauce, including enough olive oil to make a dropping but not too liquid sauce. Taste and adjust the flavours as you want.

Beach & Street Food

This is really easy and I'm dedicating it to my student friends everywhere because it's fast, and it's cool. You'll need a dozen wooden skewers.

lamb, pepper and pineapple kebabs

Makes 10–12 kebabs

175ml (6fl oz) pineapple juice
4 tbsp malt vinegar
115g (4oz) molasses sugar
salt and pepper
750g (1lb 10oz) lamb neck fillet,
   trimmed and cut into 3cm
   (1¼in) chunks

2 large red peppers, deseeded
2 large green peppers, deseeded
2 red onions
1 fresh pineapple
3 large bananas (not too ripe)
sunflower or groundnut oil,
   for brushing

1. Wash the meat and pat it dry with kitchen paper. Mix the pineapple juice, vinegar, sugar and seasoning together. Put the lamb into a bowl and pour half the marinade over it. Cover and put in the fridge for an hour or up to 4 hours.

2. Soak the wooden skewers in cold water for at least 30 minutes before cooking the kebabs to help prevent them from burning.

3. Cut the peppers and onions into cubes about 3cm (1¼in) square. Remove the skin from the pineapple (cut it off with a sharp knife), quarter the fruit lengthways and remove and discard the hard central core from each piece. Cut the pineapple flesh and the banana into similar-sized chunks.

4. Thread the peppers, onions, pineapple, banana and meat evenly on to the soaked skewers to make 10–12 generously laden kebabs.

5. Heat a griddle pan until very hot, and brush the kebabs with oil. Put the kebabs on to the pan, turning frequently and using the remaining marinade for basting. They should be done in about 10 minutes. Alternatively, cook over a hot barbecue or under a preheated medium-hot grill, turning regularly.

This dish is full of what is good to eat and good for you. All parts of the lime – juice, rind and leaves – are used in the Caribbean for ailments such as colds and flu, and the angostura bitters remind me of bitter aloes. In the past, I've tended to use angostura bitters in cakes, but it is also excellent in this savoury dish.

sweet lime and angostura bitters chicken bits

Serves 4

12 chicken pieces (wings, thighs and drumsticks)
boiled rice and salad (such as Pineapple, Avocado, Orange and Mint Salad with Ginger Dressing, see page 107), to serve

FOR THE MARINADE
6 tbsp lime marmalade
juice of 1 lime

½ tbsp angostura bitters
1 tbsp soft light brown sugar
leaves from 3 sprigs of thyme
2 garlic cloves, finely chopped
1 tsp ground ginger
salt and pepper

1. Mix all the marinade ingredients together. Pierce the chicken pieces all over with a small, sharp knife. Spread the marinade all over the chicken, tucking it down into the cuts. If you can, cover and leave for a couple of hours in the fridge, turning the chicken over several times.

2. Preheat the oven to 190°C/375°F/gas mark 5. Put the chicken in an ovenproof dish. Roast in the preheated oven for about 40 minutes, spooning the juices back up over the chicken as it cooks. The chicken is ready when the juices run clear when a skewer is pushed into the thickest point.

3. Serve with rice and a salad – Pineapple, Avocado, Orange and Mint Salad with Ginger Dressing would be great on the side.

As an alternative to the kebab, we have the 'kickbab', my Caribbean version of a popular street food. You can add whatever you like to this but my version will always include some melting orange cheese. You can make the loco breads a day in advance and warm them through before stuffing with the chicken.

chicken kickbabs

Makes 8

4 boneless, skinless chicken breasts
1 x quantity Jerk Rub (*see* page 88)
1 x quantity Loco Bread dough
    (*see* page 124) or 4 pitta breads
¼ x quantity My Special Tomato Sauce
    (*see* page 125)

50g (1¾oz) Double Gloucester or
    Red Leicester cheese, grated
4 butterhead lettuce leaves, washed
    and dried (optional)
extra chopped chilli (optional if you
    want a bit more kick to your kickbab)

1. Cover the chicken with the jerk rub and leave to marinate in the fridge, covered, ideally for a few hours or overnight.

2. Roll and fold the loco breads, according to the instructions (*see* page 124). Preheat the oven to 220°C/425°F/gas mark 7, putting 2 shallow baking trays in the oven to heat up.

3. Put the breads in the oven on one of the baking trays along with the chicken on the other. Cook the breads for 10–15 minutes. Cook the chicken for 12–15 minutes, turning them over once, until the juices run clear when you pierce the flesh at the thickest point with a skewer. Cool the breads a little on a wire rack.

4. Slice the chicken and stuff one pocket of loco bread with half a chicken breast. Top with the tomato sauce. In the other pocket put some grated cheese and a bit of torn lettuce, if you'd like some greenery, and some chopped chilli if you want them really kicking! Serve straight away and give each person 2 kickbabs. (If using pitta breads, stuff each pitta with some chicken, sauce, cheese, lettuce and chilli.) Eat up!

This is a great snack – two bites and you're done. Have it with a fresh, fruity smoothie and dip them in chilli or hot sauce if you want to whack up the heat. You can make the batter in the morning for the evening if you want, but don't leave it in the fridge for longer than that.

shrimp and corn cakes

Makes 20–25 cakes

50g (1¾oz) fine cornmeal or polenta
50g (1¾oz) plain flour
250g (9oz) sweetcorn, canned or frozen (drained if canned, defrosted if frozen)
3 large free range eggs
80ml (2½fl oz) milk
40g (1½oz butter), melted and cooled
salt and pepper
175g (6oz) cooked peeled prawns

2 spring onions, green part only, chopped
sunflower or groundnut oil for frying

TO SERVE
hot sauce
extra fresh coriander leaves
3 limes, cut into wedges
small tub of sour cream

1. Simply put all the ingredients – except the prawns, spring onions and frying oil – into a food processor and whizz, using the pulse button so that the corn gets chopped rather than puréed. Add the prawns and spring onions and mix everything together.

2. Heat 2 tbsp sunflower or groundnut oil in a frying pan and, once it's hot but not smoking, spoon 1 tbsp dollops of the batter into the pan. Once each cake has set underneath, flip it over and cook until golden on the other side. It should take about 3 minutes on each side. Add more oil as and when you need to.

3. Drain on kitchen paper and serve with your choice of hot sauce, sprigs of coriander, lime wedges and dollops of sour cream for dipping.

I call floury potatoes 'Irish potatoes'. Being more of a rarity than the normal sweet potatoes in the Caribbean, they were regarded as a delicacy when I was growing up. This recipe uses both types.

sweet potato and prawn cakes with avocado salsa

Serves 6–8

1 kg (2lb 4 oz) sweet potatoes
500g (1lb 2oz) King Edward potatoes, peeled and cut into large chunks
6 tbsp sunflower or groundnut oil
1 onion, finely chopped
1 red and 1 green chilli, deseeded and finely chopped
4 garlic cloves, finely chopped
3 tsp ground cumin
salt and pepper
250g (9oz) cooked peeled prawns, cut into chunks if they are very big
leaves from 1 small bunch of fresh coriander, finely chopped
5 tbsp plain flour, plus extra for coating

FOR THE SALSA
2 avocados, roughly chopped
200g (7oz) well-flavoured tomatoes, deseeded and finely chopped
1 tsp ground cumin
1 garlic clove, finely chopped
2 spring onions, finely chopped
2 red chillies, deseeded and finely chopped
juice of ½ lime
4 tbsp olive oil
West Indian hot sauce, to taste
salt and pepper

1. Preheat the oven to 190°C/ 375°F/gas mark 5. Bake the sweet potatoes until completely tender – about 30 minutes for skinny ones and 45 minutes to 1 hour for large ones. Test for tenderness with the point of a knife. Boil the King Edwards until tender. Drain and leave to cool. When all the potatoes are cool enough to handle, remove the skin and discard.

2. Heat 1½ tbsp of the oil in a frying pan and sauté the onion and chilli until soft but not coloured. Add the garlic and cumin and cook for another 2 minutes to release the smell of the spice. Mash this together with the sweet potato flesh, ordinary potato flesh, salt and pepper, prawns and coriander. Add the flour and incorporate it. Taste the mixture to check the seasoning, cover it, then put it in the fridge to firm up a little.

3. With floured hands, form the mixture into patties a little smaller than a burger – it will make about 16. You should be able to bring the mixture together in your hands without it falling apart – gradually add more flour if it is very loose. The mixture will be sticky but it will work once you get it into the pan. Give each cake a light coating of flour. If you're making these in advance (and it's a good idea), put the patties on a baking sheet, cover with clingfilm and keep in the fridge.

4. Make the salsa no more than 30 minutes before you want to serve it, otherwise the avocado can go a sludgy green colour. Mix all the ingredients together and cover the salsa.

5. Heat some of the remaining oil in a frying pan and fry the cakes until golden and hot through – about 3–4 minutes a side. You'll have to do them in batches. Add more oil as you need it. Keep the cooked ones warm in a low oven and, when they're all ready, serve immediately with the salsa.

Patties are great Caribbean street food, not so very far from a Cornish pasty as an idea – both are meals in a casing you can carry and eat – so you can make patties or a dubbed-up version of a pasty using this recipe. The quantity you make is up to you: four is big enough for lunch for four average people and three enough for three big Cornish appetites.

smoked fish and lime patties

Makes 3–4 patties, depending on what size you want

FOR THE FILLING
300ml (½ pint) milk
250g (9oz) smoked haddock
50g (1¾oz) butter
1 large onion, finely chopped
1 garlic clove, finely chopped
1 tbsp plain white flour
½ red chilli, deseeded
70g (2½oz) frozen peas
zest of 1-2 limes

FOR THE PATTY PASTRY
225g (8oz) plain flour
1½ tsp ground turmeric
pinch of salt
115g (4oz) cold butter, cut into
  small cubes
½ egg, lightly beaten, to glaze

1. Put the milk and haddock into a wide pan and bring to a simmer. Poach for 5 minutes. Remove the fish from the pan (keep the milk) and flake, discarding any skin and bones. Melt the butter in a frying pan and in it gently cook the onion and garlic until soft. Sprinkle on the flour and stir for a minute or two. Add the warm fish-poaching milk gradually, stirring after each addition to get a smooth sauce. Stir in the chilli and peas. Add lime zest, to taste. Gently fold in the cooked fish and leave to cool completely.

2. Put the flour, turmeric and salt in a bowl and rub in the butter. Add 4–5 tbsp water and mix. Roll into a ball and chill for 30 minutes. Preheat the oven to 200°C/400°F/gas mark 6.

3. Cut the pastry into 3 or 4 pieces, depending on whether you want larger or smaller patties. Roll the first piece out into a large oval about ½cm (¼in) thick. Put a quarter of the filling (or a third, if making 3 patties) in the middle, leaving about 4cm (1½in) around the edge. Brush the edge with water. Fold the pastry over lengthways and use a fork to crimp the edges.

4. Prick the patties or pasties with the fork, brush with the beaten egg and cook in the preheated oven for 25 minutes or until nice and golden brown.

Levi's tip: If making a rough-and-ready Caribbean version of a pasty, put the filling in the middle of the rolled-out pastry, pull the pastry together on top and pinch together to form a ridge from end to end.

These are really easy and fun and great with chilli dipping sauce, or use Sauce Chien (*see* page 92). Don't be put off by the deep-frying; it is easy to do at the last minute if you take a little care.

prawn acras

Serves 8 as a starter or nibbles with drinks

500g (1lb 2oz) raw tiger prawns
200g (7oz) plain flour
250ml (9fl oz) water
1 tsp baking powder
1 tbsp very finely chopped flat-leaf parsley
3 spring onions, green part only, finely chopped

2 shallots, very finely chopped
2 garlic cloves, very finely chopped
1 hot red chilli (ideally Scotch bonnet), deseeded and finely chopped
salt and pepper
1 litre (1¾ pints) sunflower or groundnut oil for deep-frying
flaked sea salt

1. Pull the heads off the prawns and remove the little legs. (You can either discard these trimmings or use them to make fish stock.) With a sharp knife, make a shallow cut down the back of each prawn and, with your finger or a cocktail stick, remove and discard the black vein. If the prawns are very large, cut them in half.

2. Mix everything else – except the oil and sea salt – together and beat until you have a smooth paste. Add the prawns, mix, cover and leave for 30 minutes.

3. Heat the oil until very hot – it should come no more than halfway up the side of your chosen pan. Be very careful and don't leave the pan unattended. Drop teaspoonfuls of the mixture into the oil and fry until dark golden – little fritters will form and rise to the top of the oil. Drain on kitchen paper and sprinkle with sea salt. Serve immediately.

Sweet potatoes are a staple in the Caribbean and this is one of the simplest ways to cook them. It's real no-fuss fast food: just bake the potato and bung in the saltfish and okra. Those who like sweet and salty flavours together will love this dish. You could use smoked haddock instead if you like, which will avoid the saltfish soaking process.

saltfish and okra stuffed sweet potato

Serves 2

2 sweet potatoes
250g (9oz) saltfish
2 tbsp sunflower or groundnut oil
½ red pepper, deseeded and finely diced
½ green pepper, deseeded and finely diced
1 spring onion, chopped
1 garlic clove, finely chopped

2.5cm (1in) piece of root ginger, finely chopped
1 hot red chilli (ideally Scotch bonnet), deseeded and finely chopped
6 okra, trimmed and finely chopped
leaves from 2 sprigs of thyme
2 knobs of butter, to serve

1. Preheat the oven to 190°C/375°F/gas mark 5. Prick the sweet potatoes with a fork, wrap in foil and bake in the oven until completely tender (it will take about 40 minutes).

2. Meanwhile, make the filling. Wash the saltfish in warm water, then put it into a pan of cold water and bring to the boil. Drain, add fresh cold water to the pan, put back the saltfish and repeat the process. After draining for the second time, taste a little bit of the cod and see how salty it is. If it is still too salty, bring to the boil in fresh water for a third time.

3. Heat the oil in a frying pan and put in all the vegetables and flavourings. Cook these until the peppers and onion are soft, then flake and add the saltfish. Cook for another 4 minutes or so, until everything is tender.

4. Split the cooked sweet potatoes, add a knob of butter, and spoon the filling inside. Serve immediately.

In the Caribbean, lobster is hotel food. You have to get up really early to go to the beach and get it from the fishermen before it all goes off to the restaurants. Pick a lobster that is lively and heavy for its size. This recipe is good cooked either on an inside griddle – though make sure it is really hot – or outside on a barbecue, and it's delicious with either Lime, Chilli and Coriander Butter (*see* page 64) or Lime, Chilli and Coriander Mayo (*see* page 126).

barbecued lobster

Serves 4

2 live lobsters, each about 1kg (2lb 4oz)

oil for brushing
lime or lemon wedges, to serve

1. To kill the lobsters humanely, set them one-by-one on a board in front of you, claws facing the right. On top of the lobster shell you'll see a cross just below the head. Stick the point of a sharp, heavy knife right here and push it through to the board. The lobster will be killed instantly. Now take the knife and slice right down the middle of the lobster, lengthways. Repeat with the second lobster.

2. Look at the insides. Remove and discard all the bits and bobs you see in the sac behind the eyes, then you will see little pale-coloured 'claws'. Pull those out and discard as well. Then remove and reserve the green gunge, which despite appearances is a delicacy called the tomalley, the lobster liver. (You'll need to sauté it gently if you want to eat it, as it will simply burn on the barbecue or griddle.) Treat similarly any coral sac you may find, as this is the lobster roe.

3. Remove the claws as they cook at a different rate to the rest of the lobster. Crack them by hitting them with a sharp knife to help the heat to penetrate.

4. Place the lobster claws on a searing-hot barbecue and cook for 6 minutes, then turn them and add the lobster halves, cut side down. Cook the halves for 3 minutes, then turn them over and cook for another 2 minutes. The claws take another 6 minutes on their second side, so it should all be ready together.

5. If you are using a griddle, get your griddle pan as hot as possible and paint the lobster with oil before putting it in the pan. The cooking times will be the same. The lobster will turn from bluey-black to bright orange when cooked. Serve with the lemon or lime wedges.

This reminds me of feasts at summer music festivals when I was cooking for our band. It was something easy I could do for the boys – just throwing on the garlic and cooking the prawns before we went on stage. Use Dublin Bay prawns (langoustines) if you can get them, instead of tiger prawns. Serve with Pineapple and Mint Salsa (*see* page 126), Lime, Chilli and Coriander Mayo (*see* page 126) or Caribbean Salsa Verde (*see* page 127).

barbecued prawns

Serves 6

6 tbsp olive oil
3 tbsp white wine vinegar
4 garlic cloves, finely chopped
salt and pepper

small bunch of parsley, finely chopped
24 raw tiger prawns
lemon or lime wedges, to serve

1. Mix the oil, vinegar, garlic, seasoning and parsley together. Pull the heads off the prawns and remove the little legs. (You can either discard these trimmings or use them to make fish stock.) With a sharp knife, make a shallow cut down the back of each prawn and, with your finger or a cocktail stick, remove and discard the black vein. Put the tails into the oil and vinegar mixture, cover and leave to marinate in the fridge for about an hour. Meanwhile, if you intend to cook the prawns on wooden skewers, soak these in cold water while the prawns marinate to prevent them from burning on the barbecue.

2. Remove the prawns from their marinade and cook them either on soaked wooden skewers on a very hot barbecue or under a hot grill. Alternatively, cook on a searing griddle pan. In either case, reckon on about 3 minutes each side and baste with the marinade as you go along. Serve with lemon or lime wedges and any of the lovely sauces suggested above.

Patties are as Jamaican as rice and peas and are the most widely available street food: the Jamaican fast food. This is an ital-version – Rasta style! It has no meat and uses bright, healthy vegetables and orange cheese in the yellow Jamaican patty pastry. The colour is to go with the feeling you get from them – like sunshine.

sunny vegetable patties

Makes 6–8

1 yellow pepper, deseeded and cut into 1cm (½in) dice
150g (5½oz) carrots, cut into 1cm (½in) dice
300g (10½oz) butternut squash, peeled, deseeded and cut into 1cm (½in) dice
4 tbsp chopped fresh coriander leaves
4 spring onions, finely chopped
200g can sweetcorn, drained
100g (3½oz) orange cheese (such as Double Gloucester), grated
2-4 tsp salt
1 x quantity Patty Pastry (see page 138)
½ egg, lightly beaten, to glaze

1. Preheat the oven to 200°C/400°F/gas mark 6.

2. Put the pepper, carrots and squash in a saucepan with a small amount of just-boiled water. Cover and cook for 4 minutes. Drain, put in a bowl and mix with all the other ingredients, except the pastry and beaten egg. Leave to cool completely.

3. Cut the pastry into 6 or 8 pieces, depending on whether you want larger or smaller patties. Roll the first piece out into a large circle, with the pastry about ½cm (¼in) thick. Put an eighth of the filling (or a sixth, if making 6 patties) on one side of the pastry, leaving about 1cm (½in) around the edge. Brush the edge with some of the egg glaze. Fold the other half of the pastry circle over the filled half and press the edges together to seal, using a fork to crimp the edges.

4. Brush the patties with the remaining beaten egg glaze, place on a baking sheet lined with greaseproof paper and cook in the oven for 25 minutes or until nice and golden on the outside as well as on the inside.

Preparing corn was a communal thing when I was growing up in Content and this dish reminds me of those times. Serve the corn with lashings of Lime, Chilli and Coriander Butter (*see* page 64).

barbecued corn

Serves 4

4 ears of sweetcorn
sunflower or groundnut oil
salt and pepper
Lime, Chilli and Coriander Butter
  (*see* page 64), to serve

1. If your sweetcorn is without leaves and you are in a hurry, bring a big pot of water to the boil. Add the corn and boil until just tender (about 10 minutes). Brush with oil, season and set the corn on the bars of a barbecue. Let it get a lovely charred appearance, turning it round every so often, then serve.

2. If you want to go the purist route, buy your sweetcorn with leaves on. Pull the leaves back (but not off) and pull out and discard the silky threads underneath. Fold the leaves back in place, twisting them together at the end. You won't need oil or seasoning. Wrap in foil, or cook as they are, burying them in the barbecue embers for about 40 minutes.

As a boy I'd climb the cashew trees in my grandfather's garden and eat the fruit. He thought it was the birds until one day he caught me. I fell out of the tree straight into his arms for a big telling-off.

spicy cashews

Serves 8 as a pre-supper snack

½ tbsp sunflower or groundnut oil
1 level tsp ground allspice
½ tsp pepper
1 tsp chilli flakes
½ tsp cinnamon
150g (5½oz) unsalted cashews
1–2 tsp sea salt
½ red chilli, deseeded and finely
  chopped (optional)
juice of ½ lime

1. Mix the oil with the spices and toss the cashews around in the spicy oil. Put all of this into a dry frying pan (use a spatula to get every drop of seasoning out into the pan). Cook over a medium heat, stirring occasionally, for about 3 minutes, then stir them continuously for another 3 minutes so that they don't catch and burn on the bottom of the pan.

2. Pour into a bowl and leave to cool. Toss with the sea salt and the fresh chilli, if liked, for a little extra colour and heat. Squeeze over a little lime and serve with a glass of Caribbean Wash (*see* page 187), a nice cold beer or a rum cocktail.

I've got to mention my Scottish side in this book. My real name is Keith Graham, which is Scottish, and I'm hoping there is a Scottish tartan for me to wear. And then there are all the great Scottish ingredients to try. This is another version of the 'tumpling', a knock-out type of dumpling inspired by Mike Tyson's 'tump' or thump. Veggie haggis is a new discovery for me and its spicy flavours, given some extra chilli kick, work their magic in this dish. It has the real Caribbean pulse. They go well with Caribbean Salsa Verde (*see* page 127) or Banana Sauce (*see* page 119).

mctumplings

Makes 5–6

250g (9oz) self-raising flour,
   plus extra for dusting
½ tsp cinnamon
pinch of salt
30g (1oz) butter
4 tbsp cooked vegetarian haggis
¼ hot red chilli (ideally Scotch bonnet),
   deseeded and finely chopped
2 tbsp chopped fresh coriander leaves
2 spring onions, green part only,
   finely chopped
90-125ml (3-4fl oz) water
sunflower or groundnut oil, for frying

1. Combine the flour, cinnamon and salt. Rub in the butter with your fingertips. In another bowl, crumble the veggie haggis with the chilli, coriander and spring onions, then rub this mixture into the flour. Gradually add enough water to make a dough and knead well for a few minutes on a floured work surface until firm.

2. Divide the dough into equal pieces, each about 75g (2½oz) in weight, and use your hands to knead and pat them out into circles about 9cm (3½in) in diameter and 3cm (1¼in) thick. Slightly flatten the edges. Leave these tumplings to one side for 10 minutes.

3. Pour enough oil into a small frying pan to get a depth of 1cm (½in). Heat for a couple of minutes over a medium to low heat, then fry the mctumplings, two at a time, turning them over when they are browned (they should take 4–5 minutes on each side). Drain them on kitchen paper and eat warm.

Levi's tip: Pressing down on the edges of the mctumplings – or any tumpling – means they will cook more evenly.

You've probably already got the ingredients for this simple sweet bread in your cupboard. It's easy for kids to make the dough and then you can do the frying. I've called it a 'tumpling' instead of a dumpling to go with the Tyson's Tump (*see* page 182), which you should definitely be drinking alongside it! It's delicious with savoury dishes such as fried chicken or a slice of ham, or spread with butter and jam for tea.

banana tumplings

Makes 4

250g (9oz) self-raising flour,
   plus extra for dusting
1 tsp cinnamon
2 tsp demerara sugar

30g (1oz) soft butter
1 ripe banana, mashed
100-150ml (3½-5fl oz) water
sunflower or groundnut oil, for frying

1. Combine the flour, cinnamon and sugar. Rub in the butter and stir in the banana. Gradually add enough water to make a dough and knead well for a few minutes on a floured work surface until firm.

2. Wipe down the surface and dust with more flour. Divide the dough into 4 pieces and roll each out to get circles about 10cm (4in) in diameter.

3. Pour enough oil into a small frying pan to get a depth of 1cm (½in). Heat for a couple of minutes over a medium heat and then cook the tumplings in the oil, one at a time, turning them over when they are browned (they should take about 3 minutes on each side). Drain them on kitchen paper and cool on a wire rack – though they smell so good you may want to eat them hot!

Desserts & Drinks

Here's a jelly with the colours of reggae music and Rasta culture and a trio of mouthwatering citrus flavours that will please every age, from the ancients to the young kids. Bring it to the table with a wibble-wobble-gobble! Use a 1 litre (1¾ pint) jelly mould or basin.

jamaican jelly

Serves 5–6

15 sheets of gelatine (30g/1oz in total)
200ml (7fl oz) diluted lime cordial
350ml (12fl oz) ready-made
  'fresh' lemonade
450ml (16fl oz) orange juice
  (ideally blood orange)

juice of 2 limes
6-9 tbsp caster sugar, to taste
green food colouring (optional)
juice of 1 lemon
yellow food colouring (optional)
red food colouring (optional)

1. Separate the gelatine into batches of 4, 5 and 6 sheets. Put each batch into a shallow dish of warm water (remember which is which!). Leave to soak for 5 minutes. Meanwhile, take 3 saucepans and put the cordial into one, the lemonade into the second and the orange juice into the third.

2. Add most of the lime juice to the lime cordial with 1–2 tbsp sugar. Heat gently to dissolve the sugar. Taste and adjust the sweetness; it should have a good citrus kick, so add more lime as required. Add 1–2 drops of green food colouring, if liked. Add half the lemon juice and 2–3 tbsp sugar to the lemonade. Heat gently to dissolve the sugar. Taste and adjust as before, adding a few drops of yellow food colouring, if liked. Add 3–4 tbsp sugar to the orange juice and heat gently to dissolve the sugar. Add enough red food colouring to get a good shade, if liked.

3. Squeeze out the gelatine and put the batch of 4 sheets into the lime mixture, 5 into the lemon and 6 into the orange. Stir each liquid over a gentle heat to dissolve the gelatine. This takes just a minute or so. Let the jelly mixtures cool.

4. Pour the lime mixture into the bottom of the jelly mould and put in the freezer. Meanwhile, chill the lemon mixture in the fridge. The lime jelly should set within about 30 minutes or so. Pour the lemon mixture on top and return the mould to the freezer for 30 minutes. Pour the orange on top and leave to set in the fridge. To unmould the jelly, gently run a knife around the top edge, then dip the mould very briefly in hot water. Put a plate on top and invert. Tap firmly to release the jelly. Hey presto!

Some fruits go so well together they are sweet love on a plate. That's why this Caribbean fruit salad is called Matrimony. I've made two versions here: the first uses beautiful fresh fruits; the other uses ingredients off the shelf, but is none the less loving for that.

matrimony de luxe

Serves 4

1 ripe mango
2 kiwi fruit
2 ripe passion fruit
1 large knob of preserved stem ginger
1½ tbsp ginger syrup
juice of ½ lime
ice cream or cream, to serve

1. Cut both cheeks from the mango stone and cross-hatch the flesh, making sure your knife goes right down to the skin but not through it. Press the centre of each piece of the mango skin with your fingers so that the straight, cut flesh side becomes rounded (it will look like a mango hedgehog), then use the knife to disconnect the cubes of mango. Remove from the stone any remaining mango flesh that you can reach, peel and dice it and add to the rest.

2. Peel the kiwis, cut into quarters and carefully cut out the central white core. Cut each quarter into 3 long pieces to get long, elegant slithers of fruit. Put the mango and kiwi in a serving bowl with the scooped-out flesh of the passion fruit.

3. Finely dice the preserved ginger. Scatter it over the fruit salad. Drizzle over the syrup and squeeze over the lime. Mix together carefully. Serve the Matrimony on its own, or with ice cream or cream, and enjoy the sweet rewards of bliss.

shotgun marriage

Serves 4

3 small bananas
410g can guavas, drained
200g can pineapple chunks, drained
4 tbsp condensed milk
1 capful of dark rum
good grating of nutmeg

1. Cut the bananas into slim chunks about 3cm (1¼in) wide, on the diagonal.

2. Put all the fruit into a serving bowl. Drizzle on the condensed milk and sprinkle over the rum. Grate over the nutmeg. There you have it: quick matrimony off-the-shelf – a shotgun marriage!

What a stunner this recipe is, adapted from one by the London chef Rowley Leigh. The Mango Honey Ice Cream (*see* below) works well with this.

pineapple in lime, vanilla and rum syrup

Serves 5–7

100g (3½oz) demerara sugar
150ml (¼ pint) water
1 vanilla pod
zest of 1 lime
2 tbsp rum (optional)
1 large ripe pineapple
ice cream, to serve

1. Heat the sugar and water in a saucepan gently until the sugar dissolves. Halve the vanilla pod and scrape the seeds into the pan. Add the rest of the pod and the lime zest. Simmer gently for 10–12 minutes until the liquid is reduced and syrupy. Add the rum, if liked. Soak wooden skewers in cold water for at least 30 minutes before cooking the pineapple.

2. Meanwhile, top and tail the pineapple. Cut away the skin, then cut out the spiny 'eyes'. Cut it lengthways into eighths and cut out and discard the inner core from each piece. Push the pineapple pieces on to the presoaked wooden skewers.

3. If grilling the pineapple, preheat the grill to high. Grill the skewered pineapple pieces for 8–10 minutes on a baking sheet lined with foil. Alternatively, cook for 8–10 minutes over a hot barbecue. Spoon over the hot spiced syrup and serve.

mango honey ice cream

Serves 6–8

200g (7oz) mango honey
  (or other kind)
4 large free range egg yolks
300ml (½ pint) double cream
300ml (½ pint) full-fat milk
1 tsp vanilla essence

1. Heat the honey until runny. Find a bowl that will fit over a pan of water. Beat the egg yolks and honey in the bowl and bring the pan of water to a simmer. Bring the cream and milk nearly to the boil in another pan, then pour it over the egg yolks and honey, whisking all the time.

2. Place the bowl over the pan of water (the base of the pan should not touch the water). Cook, stirring, until the custard is thick enough to coat the back of a spoon (about 10 minutes). Pour the custard through a sieve, stir in the vanilla and leave to cool, then churn in an ice-cream machine. When ready, transfer to a shallow plastic container and freeze until needed.

This looks great – like strawberries and cream –
and tastes like paradise.

boozy strawberries with coconut

Serves 4

2 tbsp caster sugar
2 tbsp orange liqueur
juice of ½ lime
200g (7oz) strawberries
½ coconut, freshly grated
   (see page 122)

1. Mix the sugar with the liqueur and lime juice. Leave for 10 minutes, stirring occasionally, and the sugar will dissolve.

2. Meanwhile, hull the strawberries and cut into quarters. Mix the coconut with the liqueur and lime mixture.

3. In 4 cocktail glasses, spoon in a layer of coconut, then one of strawberries. Repeat until all the ingredients are used up.

Whoo-hoooo! This is a recipe of beautiful tropical
fruits and flavours to share with the one you love.

passion pineapple

Serves 2

1 ripe pineapple
3 tbsp demerara sugar
3 ripe passion fruit
juice of 1½ limes
6 capfuls of dark rum

1. Carefully slice the top off the pineapple about 3cm (1¼in) down, to make a good lid to put back on later. Set it aside. Use a knife and spoon to gouge out the hard central core (discard this) and then the succulent flesh, taking care not to cut through the base or skin. Cut the flesh into small chunks.

2. Put 1 tbsp sugar in the bottom of the pineapple. Add a third of the pineapple chunks and the flesh of 1 passion fruit. Squeeze over half a lime and sprinkle on 2 capfuls of rum. Repeat twice more: sugar, pineapple, passion fruit, lime, rum. If space is tight, just leave out some of the pineapple.

3. Replace the top and put the pineapple in a bowl, just in case some of the liquid leaks out. You can eat it straight away or, ideally, leave in the fridge for 8–24 hours. When you're ready to eat it, give it a stir and serve with 2 spoons.

This is really good – fabulocious! If you keep it in the fridge you will always be opening the door for a sneaky spoonful. Lovely with pineapple or sliced mangos with lime squeezed over them.

coconut rice pudding

Serves 6

250g (9oz) short-grain rice
100g (3½oz) caster sugar
750ml (1 pint 7fl oz) full-fat milk

400ml can coconut milk
4 tbsp double cream (optional)

1. Put the rice, sugar and milk in a heavy-bottomed saucepan and heat gently until the milk is simmering.

2. Simmer the rice very gently, stirring occasionally, until it is cooked and the mixture is thick and porridge-like – it will take about 30 minutes.

3. Remove from the heat and stir in the coconut milk. It will seem too sloppy but it firms up as it cools. Once it's cool, cover it, then put it in the fridge if you want to chill it.

4. Stir in the cream, if liked, and serve.

This is gorgeous! It's even more delicious with a tablespoon of coconut-flavoured rum poured over each serving!

lime, mint and ginger sorbet

Serves 4–6

225g (8oz) granulated sugar
600ml (1 pint) water
leaves from 8 sprigs of fresh mint, plus extra to decorate
2.5cm (1in) piece of root ginger, sliced

juice of 5 limes and finely grated zest of 1
juice of ½ lemon
1 small free range egg white, beaten medium-stiff

1. Put the sugar and 225ml (8fl oz) of the water in a small saucepan and gently bring to the boil, stirring to help the sugar dissolve, then boil for 2 minutes. Remove from the heat, stir in the mint leaves and ginger and leave to get completely cold – this gives the flavours a chance to work on the syrup. Strain the syrup and add the remaining water. Mix with the lime and lemon juice and the lime zest.

2. Churn in an ice-cream machine, following the manufacturer's instructions, or pour into a broad, shallow plastic or stainless steel box and put into the freezer. If you do the latter, you'll need to tip it all into a blender and whizz it briefly, or beat the mixture really well, 3 times during the freezing process. This is to break up the crystals and make the mixture smooth. Each time, return the sorbet to the freezer and repeat the process when the mixture is more frozen.

3. Whether you are making it by hand or in an ice-cream machine, add the beaten egg white near the end of the freezing time and churn or mix by hand again – it needs to be well incorporated.

4. Serve scoops in individual bowls decorated with mint leaves.

You can make this in ramekins or shallow brûlée dishes for a stylish pudding. It will make you feel as if you are at the end of a long lunch in the sunshine with a beautiful view of a Caribbean beach and a lazy afternoon ahead.

coconut crème brûlée

Serves 4

4-6 tbsp caster sugar
4 large free range egg yolks
200ml (7fl oz) double cream

100ml (3½fl oz) canned coconut milk
(make sure this is the full-fat variety)

1. Preheat the oven to 180°C/350°F/gas mark 4.

2. Whisk 2 tbsp of the sugar with the egg yolks. Pour the cream into a pan. Give the coconut milk a stir in its can before measuring out the amount you need into the same pan. Gently heat the creams, stirring to combine, until they come to just below the boil. Pour on to the yolks and whisk together. Pour into 4 ramekins or shallow brûlée dishes.

3. Put the dishes into a roasting tin and pour enough just-boiled water from the kettle into the tray to come halfway up the sides of the dishes. Bake for 20–30 minutes, or until set. Chill.

4. Sprinkle the remaining sugar on top in an even layer (½ tbsp on each if you're using ramekins; 1 tbsp if you're using wider brûlée dishes) and grill or use a cook's blow torch to melt and caramelize the sugar.

5. Leave to cool, then put in the fridge and chill before serving.

Deliciously bad for you and a sure-fire hit! Leave the chocolate out if you like, but don't leave out the rum...

coconut, banana and chocolate bread pudding

Serves 8

300ml (½ pint) full-fat milk
300ml (½ pint) double cream
2 tsp vanilla essence
100g (3½oz) caster sugar
3 whole, large free range eggs and
  1 yolk, lightly beaten together
200g (7oz) white bread, crusts removed
butter for greasing
3 bananas, peeled and cut into
  large chunks or thick slices

35g (1¼oz) milk chocolate chunks
  or chips
rum, 4 tbsp or to taste
½ tsp ground cinnamon
30g (1oz) fresh coconut shavings from
  ½ coconut (optional)
½ tsp ground cinnamon
whipped cream, to serve

1. Heat the milk and cream together until they come to the boil. Take off the heat and add the vanilla. In a large bowl, stir the sugar into the eggs and pour the milk and cream mixture on to this, stirring all the time. Cut the bread into fat fingers – about the length of toast soldiers. Butter a deep, ovenproof dish (about the size of a piece of A4 paper) and layer in the bread along with the bananas and chocolate chips, sprinkling with rum as you go along.

2. Pour the egg and cream mixture over the layered bread through a sieve. Push the bread down under the surface of the cream mixture and then leave it to sit for 30 minutes – this gives a lighter pudding. Meanwhile, preheat the oven to 180°C/350°F/gas mark 4.

3. Put the dish in a roasting tin, pouring just-boiled water from the kettle into the tin to come halfway up the sides of the dish and put the whole thing in the oven. Cook for about 40 minutes then scatter the coconut shavings and cinnamon evenly on top. (If using fresh coconut, make shavings using a swivel-headed vegetable peeler. *See* page 122 for instructions on how to break into a coconut and lever the flesh away from the shell.) Return to the oven for a further 10 minutes, or until the top of the pudding is golden and puffy and the eggy custard is set. It will continue to cook a little more once you take it out of the oven. Leave to cool a little and serve with the cream.

Anything to do with nuts is up my street; I'm a nutty guy! These are best eaten on the day they are made. Try them with Clarendon's Mud (*see* page 183).

banana, pecan and pumpkin seed muffins

Makes 12
large muffins

280g (10oz) plain flour
1 tsp baking powder
1 tsp bicarbonate of soda
½ tsp salt
3 large ripe bananas (weighing about 450g/1lb), mashed
125g (4½oz) caster sugar

1 large free range egg, beaten
80ml (2½fl oz) full-fat milk
90ml (3fl oz) sunflower or groundnut oil
85g (3oz) pecans, halved (optional)
40g (1½oz) pumpkin seeds, plus extra for sprinkling

1. Preheat the oven to 190°C/375°F/gas mark 5.

2. Sift the flour, baking powder, bicarbonate of soda and salt into a big bowl. In a separate bowl, mix together the bananas, sugar, egg, milk and oil.

3. Now add the wet ingredients to the dry and stir until they come together to form a batter. No flour should be visible, but the mixture should still be lumpy so be careful not to overmix. Add the nuts, if using, and pumpkin seeds, and stir them in.

4. Spoon the batter into paper cases set in a muffin tray. Sprinkle the extra pumpkin seeds over the tops of the muffins, then bake for 20–25 minutes until the tops are lightly browned and springy to the touch. Cool on a wire rack.

This is 'cheeky' food: the fieriness of the fruity hot sauce and the spiced-up plantain go straight to your cheeks! As well as having these on a picnic, they can be heated up as a pudding or as a party dish to feed a crowd.

plantain pies

Makes 8

3 large, very ripe plantain
100g (3½oz) caster sugar, plus
   4 tsp to sprinkle on top
½ tsp grated nutmeg
1 tsp vanilla essence
½ tsp cinnamon
2 x 225g pieces of ready-rolled
   shortcrust pastry
plain flour, to dust
8 tbsp Banana Sauce
   (see page 119)
beaten egg, to seal
milk, to glaze
cream, to serve

1. Peel the plantain and cut it into chunks. Boil until very tender (at most, this should take 10 minutes).

2. Transfer the plantain to a bowl and add the sugar, nutmeg, vanilla and cinnamon. Mix until smooth. I love this bit – it smells brilliant.

3. Put the pastry on a floured board. Cut each piece into 4 equal-sized rectangles (each about 15 x 12cm/6 x 4½in). With the long sides of each piece of pastry facing you, divide the plantain paste between the rectangles, putting it in a line lengthways across each one, just above the centre, stopping 1cm (½in) before each end. Dollop 1 tbsp of the Banana Sauce beside the plantain in each pie, again across the centre of each rectangle.

4. Brush the outside of each rectangle with beaten egg and fold the pastry over to make a closed pie, pinching the edges together to seal them well. Chill, covered, for 15–30 minutes in the fridge while you preheat the oven to 200°C/400°C/ gas mark 6.

5. Place the pies on to a piece of greaseproof paper on a baking sheet. Brush over the tops with a little fresh milk.

6. Prick each with a fork and sprinkle with caster sugar. Bake for 25–30 minutes or until the tops are golden brown. Best served warm – with cream, of course!

We have this every Christmas. The best bit is when you add in all the rum and let the fruit soak for days, knowing it's going to taste so good. This is quite dark in colour and also called black cake, because it used to be made with burnt sugar.

caribbean christmas cake

Makes 1 cake

250g (9oz) currants
250g (9oz) raisins
150g (5½oz) no-soak pitted prunes, quartered
115g (4oz) cut mixed peel
300ml (½ pint) dark rum, plus 4 tbsp extra for soaking the cake
250g (9oz) softened butter, plus extra for greasing
200g (7oz) dark soft brown sugar
5 free range eggs, lightly beaten
250g (9oz) self-raising flour
50g (1¾oz) blanched almonds, roughly chopped (leave lots of big chunks)
1½ tsp ground mixed spice
1 tsp vanilla extract

FOR THE FRUIT TOPPING
4 tbsp apricot jam
1 tbsp dark rum
20-24 no-soak pitted prunes
16-20 no-soak stoned apricots
16-24 glacé cherries, coloured if liked
9-12 no-soak dried figs
50g blanched almonds

1. Put the dried fruit and mixed peel in a saucepan and cover with rum. Bring to the boil, stir, then immediately turn off the heat. Cover and leave the fruit to macerate in the rum either overnight or up to 2 days, stirring from time to time.

2. Preheat the oven to 160°C/325°F/gas mark 3. Grease and line a 25cm (10in) round cake tin with a double layer of greaseproof paper.

3. Cream together the butter and sugar in a large bowl until pale, then beat in the eggs a little at a time, adding 1 tbsp of the flour after each addition until smooth and creamy. Beat in the remaining flour. Stir in the almonds, spice and vanilla extract followed by the fruit. Mix well, adding a couple of spoonfuls of rum if the mixture is too stiff – it should easily fall off the back of the spoon but should not be too runny.

4. Spoon the mixture into the prepared tin, cover loosely with foil and bake for about 2 hours. Remove the foil 30 minutes before the end of cooking time. The cake is ready when a skewer inserted into the centre comes out clean. While the cake is still warm, make holes all over it with a skewer and pour over the 4 tbsp rum. Leave to cool in the tin overnight, then turn the cake out. Decorate and serve immediately, or wrap in foil and keep for up to 1 week before decorating.

5. To decorate, heat the apricot jam and rum until they are mixed together, then brush some of this glaze on to the surface of the cake. Arrange the topping on the cake, either in circles or rows. Brush the fruit very generously with the rest of the glaze, so that the top is shiny. Leave to cool and store in a tin in a dark place. Eat within a week.

Kids love crumble, and you don't need to worry because any alcohol will be cooked out of the rum in this version, leaving only the gorgeous flavour. Crumble was one of my favourite puddings when I came to school in London. And you've got to serve it with custard or cream: that's the rule.

apple and rum crumble

Serves 5–6

4 cooking apples, peeled, cored
   and cut into medium chunks
30g (1oz) butter
2 tbsp dark brown muscovado sugar
5 tbsp rum
1 tsp ground ginger
good pinch of cinnamon
1 tbsp plain flour
custard or cream (or both), to serve

FOR THE TOPPING
200g (7oz) butter, cut into small
   pieces, plus 30g (1oz) to dot on top
200g (7oz) plain flour
pinch of salt
100g (3½oz) dark brown
   muscovado sugar

1. Preheat the oven to 200°C/400°F/gas mark 6.

2. Put the apples into a little simmering water and cook for 5 minutes, or 10 if you want the apple to be softer. Meanwhile, make the crumble topping. To do this in a food processor, put all the ingredients in the processor bowl and pulse until you have a breadcrumb texture. To make the topping by hand, rub the butter into the flour and salt until you have a breadcrumb texture, then stir in the sugar.

3. Drain the apples. Smear butter around a wide ovenproof dish (about the size of a piece of A4 paper is perfect) that gives plenty of space for the delicious crumble topping. Put the apples in the dish. Sprinkle over the muscovado sugar, rum, ginger, cinnamon and flour and stir them roughly into the apples. Spread the crumble topping over in an even layer. Dot with the remaining butter.

4. Put on a baking sheet in the oven for 35–45 minutes, until slightly brown on top, and serve with custard or cream.

At lots of the schools that I visit to give talks, kids bring me their chocolate brownies both as a present and to show what they can make, so I'm lucky enough to taste many different kinds! Lots of them are fab, but I have come up with the ultimate Caribbean version of this classic. Enjoy!

ginger, pecan and rum chocolate brownies

Makes about
20 brownies

250g (9oz) plain chocolate
(70 per cent cocoa solids),
broken into squares
250g (9oz) butter
5 free range eggs
350g (12oz) dark muscovado sugar

1-2 tbsp rum (optional)
150g (5½oz) plain flour, sifted
125g (4½oz) pecans, roughly chopped
4 knobs of preserved stem ginger,
cut into small pieces
sifted icing sugar, to decorate (optional)

1. Preheat the oven to 180°C/350°F/gas mark 4. Line a 30 x 20cm (12 x 8in) brownie or cake tin, 4–5cm (1½–2in) deep, with greaseproof paper.

2. Melt the chocolate and butter together in a pan over simmering water. Leave to cool slightly.

3. Whisk the eggs and sugar together, using either a hand whisk or an electric whisk, for about 5 minutes until nice and thick. Whisk in the chocolate and butter mixture, then the rum, if liked. Fold in the flour, then the nuts and ginger. Pour into the lined tin.

4. Bake the brownies for 20–25 minutes, until mostly cooked but still leaving a slightly gooey trace when you insert a knife into the middle.

5. Leave to cool slightly, then cut into triangles or small squares. Decorate by dusting with a little icing sugar, if liked.

I call this a 'contented' pudding both because I come from
Content, Jamaica, and because after eating it you'll feel that way!
You must watch the clock, but if you find you've cooked them a
little too long they will still taste great. You'll get better and better
at timing them with each attempt, which is a good excuse to
make them often...

my contented chocolate puddings

Serves 6

FOR THE CREAM
150ml (¼ pint) whipping or
   double cream
2 tbsp icing sugar
2 tbsp rum, or to taste

FOR THE PUDDINGS
75g (2¾oz) unsalted butter,
   plus extra for greasing ramekins
6 tsp cocoa powder
75g (2¾oz) chocolate, 70 per cent
   cocoa solids, broken in pieces, plus
   12 small squares for the filling
3 whole free range eggs
3 free range egg yolks
145g (5¼oz) caster sugar
75g (2¾oz) plain flour, sifted
icing sugar, to serve (optional)

1. Whip the cream into soft folds, then stir in the icing sugar
and rum and mix well. Taste and add more sugar or rum if
you want. Cover and store in the fridge.

2. Butter the insides of 6 ramekins, each about 8½cm (3½in)
across. Put 1 tsp of cocoa powder in each and roll the ramekin
around so that the cocoa powder sticks to the butter. Shake
out any excess. Preheat the oven to 160°C/325°F/gas mark 3.

3. Melt the butter and the chocolate in a bowl set over a pan
of simmering water. (The bottom of the bowl shouldn't touch
the water.) Stir to help it along, then remove the bowl and
leave to cool for 10 minutes.

4. Beat the eggs, yolks and caster sugar until pale and foamy.
Stir the chocolate mixture into the eggs, mixing well. Fold in
the flour with a metal spoon. Pour half the batter into the
ramekins, pop 2 squares of chocolate into each, then top up
with the remaining batter. Set them on a baking sheet and
put in the oven for 20–23 minutes. You need to judge when
the centre is still molten but the rest is set. Start checking at
about 20 minutes. The top will be set but still soft.

5. If you want to turn out the puddings, run a fine knife
between the pudding and its ramekin, then invert them on
to plates. For an easier life, just leave them in their pots.

6. Sift some icing sugar over the top, if liked, and serve with
the rum cream – they taste even more lovely if you break the
top of your pudding open and spoon rum cream inside.

A nice cup of tea with a big slice of my ginger cake should sort anybody out in the evening – or at any time of day. The icing gives a nice tartness.

sticky ginger cake with lime icing

Serves 8–10

115g (4oz) butter, plus extra for greasing
115g (4oz) soft dark brown sugar (preferably unrefined)
115g (4oz) treacle
55g (2oz) preserved stem ginger, chopped
225g (8oz) plain flour, sifted
1½ tsp ground ginger

2 large free range eggs, beaten
2-3 tbsp milk
½ tsp bicarbonate of soda

FOR THE ICING
juice of 1½ limes
200g (7oz) icing sugar, sifted
2 knobs of preserved stem ginger

1. Preheat the oven to 160°C/325°F/gas mark 3. Butter and base-line a 18cm (7in) cake tin. Melt the butter, sugar and treacle in a heavy-bottomed saucepan over a low heat, stirring occasionally. Don't let it boil. When it's all melted and well combined, leave to cool a little and add the stem ginger.

2. Put the flour and ground ginger into a bowl and make a well in the centre. Put the beaten eggs and treacle mixture into the well and, using a wooden spoon, gradually mix the dry ingredients into the wet ones. Be careful to get a smooth batter. Mix the milk with the bicarbonate of soda and add that too.

3. Pour the batter into the cake tin and bake in the preheated oven for 1½ hours. When cooked, a skewer inserted into the centre of the cake should come out clean. Don't open the oven door during cooking or the cake will sink a little.

4. Remove the cake from the oven and leave it in the tin for 15 minutes or so, then turn it out on to a wire rack to cool. If you need to keep the cake – and it will actually taste better after a few days – then wrap it in foil or greaseproof paper, but don't ice until the day you want to eat it.

5. To make the icing, add the lime juice to the icing sugar and stir until smooth. Leave it for a while to firm up. Now you can choose either to cover the top of the cake completely with icing, or drizzle it on with the tines of a fork. Cut the stem ginger into very fine, wafer-thin slivers and scatter those on top.

With the very sweet topping merged with the carrots and ginger, this is a great recipe for a very moist carrot cake.

carrot cake

Serves 10

175ml (6fl oz) sunflower or groundnut oil, plus extra for greasing
175g (6oz) light brown muscovado sugar
3 large free range eggs, lightly beaten
140g (5oz) grated carrots (about 3 carrots)
125g (4½oz) raisins
50g (1¾oz) chopped pecans
grated zest of 1 large orange
175g (6oz) self-raising flour

1 tsp bicarbonate of soda
1 tsp ground cinnamon
¼ tsp ground allspice
½ tsp grated nutmeg

FOR THE FROSTING
100g (3½oz) cream cheese
200g (7oz) icing sugar, sifted
juice of ½ lime
chopped pecans, to decorate

1. Preheat the oven to 180°C/350°F/gas mark 4. Oil and line the base and sides of an 18cm (7in) square cake tin with greaseproof paper.

2. Tip the sugar into a large mixing bowl, pour in the oil and add the eggs. Mix with a wooden spoon, then stir in the grated carrots, raisins, nuts and orange zest.

3. Mix the flour, bicarbonate of soda and spices, then sift into the bowl. Lightly mix all the ingredients together – you don't want to overwork the mixture. It will be quite soft and almost runny.

4. Pour the mixture into the prepared tin and bake for 40–45 minutes or until a skewer inserted into the centre comes out clean. Cool in the tin for 5 minutes, then turn it out, peel off the paper and cool on a wire rack.

5. Meanwhile, mix the cream cheese, icing sugar and lime juice together. Put in the fridge and leave to firm up. Spread over the cake once it has cooled and scatter with the pecans. Cut the cake into oblongs or squares to serve.

This reminds me of my school days when I'd enjoy a nice ice-cold Sky Juice in a bag or pot. In the Caribbean little clear bags of it, bright and refreshing, are hung up for sale in the street. Fantastic! Add some rum and you get my adult version: Sky-high Juice! The street sellers in the Caribbean have special ice shavers but you can use ice cubes crushed up in a blender or bashed to bits in a tea towel. You want it to have a reasonably fine texture, but not slushy: it will melt soon enough.

sky juice/sky-high juice

Serves 1

150ml (¼ pint) good cordial with a
    Caribbean flavour, such as lime
    and lemongrass
3 kinds of food colouring
    (I go for green, yellow and red)
500ml (18fl oz) crushed ice
1 capful of rum, for adults

1. Put the cordial in 3 glasses and stir a few drops of different coloured food colouring into each. Put the ice into 3 bowls. Add a coloured cordial to each and stir around to mix well.

2. Put one layer of the coloured and flavoured ice in a clear freezer bag, or a big, tall glass, put the next on top, then finish with the last one. The colours will soon bleed into each other as the ice melts, but it looks great to start with.

3. If making sky-high juice, pour over the rum. Drink with a bright-coloured straw, lie back and look at the sky.

This will blow your head off...kill or cure!

jamaican cold cure

Serves 4

500ml (18fl oz) white rum
3 garlic cloves, smashed with the
    side of a knife
6 allspice berries
½ red chilli, roughly chopped
40g (1½oz) root ginger,
    roughly chopped

1. Mix everything together and leave it to steep overnight.

2. We don't usually strain this – just leave the bits in but avoid them – but you can strain it if you prefer.

Every Caribbean person knows a version of this stout punch. This one is inspired by Mike Tyson's knock-out punch; in the Caribbean, a thump is a 'tump'. You can add a bit of milk if you'd prefer it to be less alcoholic, though I wouldn't do that. It makes you happy and mellow. If you're giving it to your girlfriend or boyfriend, be sure to drink it near the bedroom – you're not going to get much further once you've had a few glassfuls of this!

tyson's tump

397g can condensed milk
4 x 284ml bottles stout
170g can evaporated milk
1 cinnamon stick, halved
a little grated nutmeg
6 whole cloves (or ¼ tsp ground)
2 tsp vanilla essence
few drops almond essence, to taste
6 tbsp rum, or to taste

Serves 8 (or maybe even fewer!)

1. Put the condensed milk in a large bowl and slowly add the stout and evaporated milk, stirring all the time until smooth, then add everything else and mix it well. It's good to leave this to mellow in the fridge for a couple of hours, so the spices can really jazz up the flavour of the stout.

2. To serve, ladle into tall glasses filled with ice.

You can add strong, cold coffee to this cocktail instead of coffee liqueur to make a longer, less potent drink, if you like.

jamaican brown cow

Serves 1

125ml (4fl oz) coffee liqueur,
   such as Tia Maria
125ml (4fl oz) evaporated milk
1 capful of rum, or to taste
juice of ½ lime
ice cubes
ground coffee or a few chocolate-
   covered coffee beans, to garnish

1. Shake all the liquids together in a cocktail shaker and pour over ice. Top with a sprinkling of ground coffee or the chocolate-covered beans and serve right away.

Clarendon is the parish where I grew up and this is one of my favourite recipes. You can use it in so many ways. You can drink it like a smoothie or serve it as a sauce – it's great with the Caramel-Lime Chicken (*see* page 35) and other brown-down dishes.

clarendon's mud

Serves 4 as a drink or 8 as a dip

35g (1¼oz) root ginger,
   roughly chopped
1½ avocado pears, flesh only
1 ripe mango, flesh only
6 tbsp condensed milk
¼ tsp ground cloves
⅓ whole nutmeg, freshly grated
juice of ½ lime
4 tbsp coconut cream
2 tbsp rum
2 tbsp roughly chopped cashew nuts

1. Put all the ingredients, except the nuts, into a blender and whizz until completely smooth. Chill the mixture in the fridge, covered, until needed.

2. Sprinkle the cashew nuts on top and, if using as a drink, serve over ice.

A coconut has three eyes on the top. Only one is a true opening, through which will emerge the shoot that will make a new coconut tree. Kids in the Caribbean play a game to guess which is the right eye; it's also the only hole that will lead them to the coconut water, and the person who guesses right gets to drink it! We call the water 'heart juice' because it is so good for you. As well as drinking it straight up, it is delicious with ice and mint.

heart juice

Serves 1

1 coconut
ice cubes
sprig of mint

1. Use a small, sharp knife to find the true hole in the top of the coconut. Dig into it and pour out the delicious coconut water into a glass.

2. Add the ice and mint. Drink deep and feel good.

The grated nutmeg in this gives it a really fantastic and refreshing sunshine taste.

coconut milk and honey smoothie

Serves 4

2½ ripe bananas, sliced
35g (1¼oz) root ginger, chopped
½ tsp ground allspice
½ tsp ground cloves
⅓ whole nutmeg, grated
400ml can coconut milk
4 tbsp condensed milk
2 tbsp runny honey
½ tsp almond essence
1 tsp vanilla essence
4 tbsp Jamaican rum
juice of 1 lime

1. Put the bananas, ginger, allspice, cloves, nutmeg and coconut milk into a blender and whizz until smooth.

2. Transfer to a bowl and stir in the condensed milk, honey, almond, vanilla, rum and lime juice. Put in the fridge to chill and serve over ice in a tall glass.

This is what you ask for when you're a kid in the Caribbean and you're thirsty. It's just sugar water with lime, really, and the old folks call it a 'wash'. It's a wonderful thirst-quencher.

caribbean wash

Serves 3–4

1 tbsp runny honey
4 tbsp demerara sugar
juice of 5 limes
300ml (½ pint) water
1 cinnamon stick, broken in half

1. Mix all the ingredients together, starting with the honey and sugar and gradually adding the liquids to make sure everything's thoroughly blended. Taste to see whether you need more water or sugar.

2. Give it all a good stir to help the cinnamon release its flavour and leave in the fridge, covered, for a couple of hours so the flavour can infuse even more (the demerara should dissolve in this time). Stir, pour over crushed ice and serve.

As a child I spent hours looking up at the blue sky and seeing the planes that flew over Content, knowing one day I'd be on one of them: where was one of those great iron birds going to take me?

blue sky/pale blue sky

Serves 1

FOR BLUE SKY
6 tbsp blue curacao
3 tbsp white rum
3 tbsp lime juice

FOR PALE BLUE SKY
1 tbsp blue curacao
1 tbsp cointreau
4 tbsp white rum
1½ tbsp single cream
2 tbsp coconut cream
juice of ½ lime
½ tsp sugar (optional)

1. For both drinks, just shake all the ingredients in a cocktail shaker over ice.

2. Serve in a chilled cocktail glass, lie back, look up at the sky and dream of summer!

beef stock

Makes about 2.5
litres (4½ pints)

900g (2lb) beef bones
1 tbsp sunflower or groundnut oil
1 onion, halved (skin on)
2 carrots, cut into large chunks

small handful of parsley
2 bay leaves
8 black peppercorns

1. Preheat the oven to 200°C/400°F/gas mark 6.

2. Put the bones on a baking sheet and place in the oven to roast for about
45 minutes, shaking the sheet once or twice during that time. They should
turn a lovely golden brown.

3. Heat the oil in a large pan and brown the onion and carrots, but don't let
them burn. When the bones are brown add them to the pan with all the other
ingredients. Cover with cold water and bring to the boil. Skim the scum that rises
to the surface (you won't get it all so don't worry too much), then turn the heat
down and simmer, uncovered, for 4 hours, skimming and adding more water
every so often.

4. Strain, cool, cover and refrigerate, then lift the fat from the surface before using.

chicken stock

Makes about 2.5 litres (4½ pints)

750-900g (1lb 10oz-2lb) chicken bones and flesh (either the carcass and bones of a cooked bird, or raw wings, bones and carcasses)
1 onion, halved (skin on)

2 sticks of celery, roughly chopped
1 large carrot, cut into large chunks
8 black peppercorns
small handful of parsley

1. Put everything into a big saucepan, cover generously with water and bring slowly to the boil. Skim off any scum that rises to the surface (you won't get it all so don't worry too much).

2. Turn the heat down to a simmer and cook, uncovered, for 3 hours, skimming and adding more water every so often. The liquid should reduce to half its original quantity.

3. Strain, cool, cover and refrigerate, then lift the fat from the surface before using. To make the flavour more intense, simply boil to reduce.

vegetable stock

Makes about 1.4 litres (2½ pints)

2 carrots, roughly chopped
2 onions, quartered
2 sticks of celery, roughly chopped
½ bulb of fennel, roughly chopped
stalk from a head of broccoli, chopped

8 button mushrooms, halved
2 tomatoes, halved
8 black peppercorns
1 bay leaf
small handful of parsley stalks

1. Put all the ingredients into a large pan and cover with water. Bring to the boil. Turn the heat down to a simmer and cook, uncovered, for 30 minutes adding more water every so often. Strain, cool, cover and refrigerate.

2. To make the flavour more intense, simply boil to reduce.

index

acknowledgements

Thanks to Hattie and Diana, Teja Picton-Howel, Borra, Rodney
and Natasha, Becca, Justine, Sara, Pene, Leanne, Wendy, Chris
and all my BBC TV crew.

One love
Levi Roots